PHD to Ph. D.:

Po H# on Dope

How Education Saved My Life

"If Zora Neale Hurston had a god-daughter, she could be Elaine Richardson: on so many paths, she comes to these pages a deep student of life—the one who studies it up close, unguarded, and, with a musician's ear for the song that lives in all of her experience, brings home its truths in their fearsome and freeing power. This book, like the life it describes, is a work of spirit Richardson records for us, another way to talk to, and talk about, God."

—*Ted Lardner, Professor of English, Cleveland State University*

"Elaine Richardson's autobiographical memoir, powerfully and eloquently written, reflects the tradition of the literary bildungsroman. Her book is a must-read for all those concerned about the social and educational crises in Black communities, particularly among Black girls and women. She holds nothing back in this story of her life in the world of pimps and ho's and the magnetizing pull of drug addiction. She rose to the ranks of boss ho, getting "White Girl pay," and she was arrested over 200 times. Dr. Richardson, aka Dr. E, neither glorifies nor sensationalizes this former life. Rather PHD to Ph.D. presents the raw, uncut truth of that life which held a grip on Elaine from the age of thirteen (and her first pregnancy) until she was in her late twenties. Her story is that of many thousands gone and the still-lingering effects of colorism and linguistic shame, that has left its mark on both women and men in our communities—the legacy of the African Holocaust, neo-enslavement and US apartheid. Elaine's inspirational life and this narrative account represent the triumph of the human spirit and the indomitable Will to survive–and thrive–"against all odds" (as Tupac would have put it). Rising from the ashes of poverty and the debilitating effects of street life, she has become an award-winning scholar and champion of the African American quest for literacy and freedom."

—*Dr. Geneva Smitherman, University Distinguished Professor, Emerita*
English and African American and African Studies
Michigan State University

PHD to Ph. D.:

Po H# on Dope

How Education Saved My Life

· · ·

Elaine Richardson, Ph.D. aka Dr. E

New City Community Press
www.newcitycommunitypress.com

Distributed by Parlor Press

ISBN: 978-0-9840429-7-5

www.newcitycommunitypress.com

Cover Design by Alex Everett

Interior Design by Elizabeth Parks

· Acknowledgements ·

H# STORIES. I never wanted anyone to hurt my daughters or hold anything over them, so I told them about myself from the time they were very young. Some of the stories were funny. Some were sad. It wasn't long before they began asking me to tell my stories to their friends. My daughters' acceptance of me gave me the courage to tell the truth about my life. I thank God for all three of you—Evelyn, Ebony and Kaila—for being my best friends, my sisters and my daughters. Thanks to my brother, Chris, my nieces Christina and Crystal, for constant encouragement, and to my Aunt Hellen Vassell.

Thanks to all the mentors and people who helped save my life: Mrs. Pauline Fullum (R.I.P), Mrs. Roberta Payne (R.I.P), Ms. Costella (R. I. P), Mrs. Janie Stanley (R.I.P), Ms. Veretta Saulsberry (R.I.P.), Ms. Betty Mitchell, Dr. Andrew Edwards, Dr. Jack Soules, Mr. Louis Brownlowe, Ms. Andrea D. Johnson, Dr. Ted Lardner, Dr. Keith Gilyard, my academic othermother—Dr. Geneva Smitherman.

Dr. Mary Weems, thank you for feedback and editorial guidance on successive drafts of the book and for encouraging me to be true to the languages of my communities. Thanks to Rhonda Crowder (Cleveland Call and Post), Charlotte Morgan, Dr. Jamila D. Smith, James Walker, Dr. Adrienne Dixson, Terrence Smith, Shelia Baylers (African American Lifestyles Magazine), Drs. Gwen Pough and Mark Anthony Neal, Dr. Adam Banks, Kevin Joy (Columbus Dispatch), Julie Cajigas (CoolCleveland.com), and Peter Lawson Jones, Judge Herbert, and Dr. Ronald Berkman, President of Cleveland State University for support. Tamara "First Lady" Allen, thanks for all you do. Alex Everett, for the cover and for being so easy to work with. You're the best! I would like to thank Elizabeth Parks for the book design. Sister dream hampton for making my dreams come true!

Thanks to my publisher, Dr. Stephen Parks, of New City Community Press, for believing in this project.

Mama and Daddy in heaven-for everything you gave to me.

I dedicate this book to everyone who has been counted out.

Contents

PHD to Ph. D.:

How Education Saved My Life

Elaine Richardson, Ph.D.

• 1 •

Where I Come From

GRANDMA TOOK MAMA OUTTA school. Her word was bond: "yuh nuh give weh pickni, yuh give weh puss and dahg." She became an instant widow, when that truck came flying around that corner and *lick* her husband dead. With five small children, one on the way, not a shilling to her name, and a 13 year-old daughter big enough to work, Mama's 6th grade teacher could beg all she wanted. She didn't have a shot in hell. Mama had all the right stuff for school, too. She was a good student, learned fast, and loved to read. Plus, she was "treaten fe white," light skinned, with "good hair" just like her teacher and the teacher's niece (Mama's classmate). Mama could live with them and get a good education. This would be better for our family in the long run. But Grandma's belief stood strong as a West Indian Mahogany tree.

Mama loved the ground Granddaddy walked on. From atop his casket, down in his grave, she begged to be buried with him. But God refused. Only half of Mama's potential could be buried with him. Her eyes were closed shut for three days and reopened like a bewitched blink into her new life of hahd wuk—a wash girl, washing white and treaten fe white folks' clothes, washing bottles in a soda factory, doing every kind of "honest" work she could for little and almost nothing. With God-given intellect, mother-wit, half of her potential, zero "oppachunity," and the collective wisdom of Jamaican sufferers, Mama learned. For every occasion of life, Mama dished out the proper bits of wisdom to me, covered in artless artful sayings and stories with simple but perfect language that I tried desperately to dismiss.

Self preservation: "If yuh give weh yuh ahss you will shit trough yuh ribs."

Racism and success: "You cyan reach noweh widout white mon han inna hit and yuh cyan dead unless nigga han inna hit." (You can't go too far in life without white folks.)

Work ethic: "Hahd wuk nevah kill nobody."

Life Consequences: "If yuh cyan hear, yuh will feel." (If you can't hear...)

Values: "Shame chree dead." (Shame tree is the spirit of self-worth inside you. Shame chree dead is said when that spirit is broken.)

Mama had to move to Kingston to work. She saved her earnings to send back down country to the rest of the family as often as she could for years. She also found time to make lifelong friends, Novlette, Merlos, and Nadine, who shared her love of ambition, knowledge, poetry, and music. Mama's favorite poet was Omar Khayyam. Her favorite musician became my Daddy. One evening, at the end of one of his Kingston concerts, Merlos and her friend Gladstone introduced Daddy to Mama. Daddy must have hit the right note because after that, their cross-country courting was on! Daddy needed a steady J. O. B. to have a family. He knew some Italians that hired him as a tailor's assistant in The Old Arcade in downtown Cleveland, and my soon to be parents got married in 1955, and Daddy brought Mama to America.

Mama saw enough sufferation in Jamaica and didn't want to add to her own by having a heap "a pickni," so she just had my brother and me. She was 38 when I was born. My folks were ole skool. Mama was born in 1921 and Daddy in 1907. "Is dat yo grandbaby?" some nosey bus rider would ask. "No." Mama would answer flatly. People called Mama "Miss Jamaica" or "Geechie Lady."

Mama sure was pretty, cute face and nice legs. I was never as pretty as Mama, but thank God, I inherited her intellect and her legs. Mama's teeth were perfect pearls. A Colgate smile, you might say. Like mine. Plus, she was a Jamaican, an uncommon Black woman in Cleveland, before it had a sizeable Jamaican population. A prize for Daddy. Check out Mama's green card:

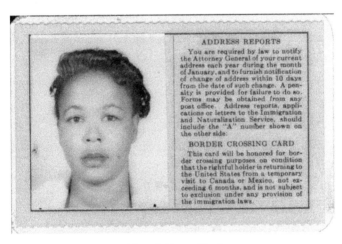

Mama's Green Card

I think my Daddy thought he was gon' control Mama. But he had another thing coming.

Mama says to Daddy:

"Give me a money fe stockin and cigarette."

"Girl, how much stockin and cigarette you need? You smokes too much."

"Chzzzz, okay, mi soon show yuh sumtimg." Mama had her own mind and her own personal goals for us and herself.

One day Mama went and got a job doing dayswork as soon as my brother and I were old enough, against Daddy's wishes. Not only did she get one job, in true Jamaican fashion, she got two! She joined the field of education, moppin and cleanin my school, Central Junior High, where she dug gum and cleaned toilets for the Cleveland Board of Education for 24 years.

Daddy didn't like the way Mama spent the money she earned. But she never buckled. "You marry me, I didn't marry you. You just pay dese bills and tek cyere uh yo kids."

Mama worked as a PBX operator by the time she met Daddy. That would be the equivalent of a telephone operator. That means her English was good enough in Jamaica to be considered Standard; however, when she applied for that position at Ohio Bell, she was told that she didn't speak English well enough. Mama wanted to go to night school; but somehow, it just never worked out.

When she could, she would read U. S. Constitution books, but she finally ditched the idea of becoming a U. S. citizen. She was a Jamaican—proud and true. When we would visit Jamaica in the summers (another thing Daddy didn't like), Mama would bargain with higglers: "Is how much?" If Mama was unhappy with the answer, she'd say "Mi is Jamaican, is how much?" She would repeat in an indignant extra patwa style 'til she got the price she wanted.

Mama did everything with us. She taught us how to pray: *Our Father which art in Heaven, hallowed be thy name…* . She taught us the ABC's and how to write our names, and a little bit of reading before we went to kindergarten. Pretty good for a lady who only went to the 6th grade. She was always fussin at us about speaking "Propah Henglish." And I hated when she would say something about my speech and make me repeat it like how "di teacha dem say it inna school." Ball games, the park, the YMCA. She took my brother to boy scouts, bought me a violin. Mama was even the PTA president.

Daddy was a short, bald- headed guy. Deep dark brown. Quiet. Dressed like James Cagney—gangsta style. When he wasn't going to work, he wore his brim broke down and carried his pool stick in a long black case. When it was cold, he used to wear this long gray tweed overcoat with padded shoulders. His pool shootin friends called him "Bullwhip shawty from section 40" or "Bullwhip" for short.

Daddy was born in Newport News, Virginia. We never knew too much about his people. His father was a man named James and he was a riveter and his mother was a woman named Olivia. She had my Daddy when she was 15 and her mother raised Daddy along with his first cousin, Shorts. Daddy told us about one cousin, who was a high school principal in Newport News named LeRoy Richardson. But the person Daddy talked about the most was his "GranMumma." He loved and feared her. "She would slap da taste out yo mouf if you disobeyed her." Daddy said she told them many a night about how the white folks used to beat her daddy back in slavery time. "Never let the white man know how you really feel" was one of Daddy's prime nuggets.

He began his love affair with music early. Learning to play trumpet as a little boy, he played in school and community orchestras. Daddy dropped out of school in the 11th grade, working in the shipyards in the port in Newport News and working as a bellhop and other odd jobs while pursuing his "better life" dream as professional musician.

Daddy's trumpet carried him all over the world. He used to tell me stuff about it, but I didn't pay any attention to the wisdom he tried to drop on me. "Don't nevah smoke no weeds, Lainey." A near fall off the bandstand one night after taking a toke off of somebody's spliff was all he needed to deter his addiction. I remember that!

Daddy around 1950 (Musician promo shot)

Though Daddy was never famous like Louis Armstrong, he played with the famous blues singer, Bessie Smith, on TOBA time. I half listened. What did he know? I later found out that TOBA was short for Theater Owners Booking Association, a network that booked Black entertainers back in the day and that my Daddy was among the first Black professional musicians.

Even after Daddy retired from being a traveling musician when he married Mama, he still practiced his trumpet every evening after dinner. He was into natural remedies, herbs, the Bible, the Black Muslims. His Black name was Gulam Jameel Abdul-Rasheed. No one knew that was Daddy's Black name, except his Muslim brothers at those meetings he attended, and my brother and me. We cracked up at that name. We didn't know any better. Daddy was also into something called Mentalphysics. He had his books and encyclopedias in a special place in the living room and couldn't nobody touch em!

Daddy didn't make friends with our neighbors the way Mama did. He didn't have time for "shiftless Negroes with nothin on they mind." He would throw a hand up to select neighbors but that was about it.

Mama said she shoulda known I was gon' be fast the way I was trying to pop out on the way to the hospital in Mr. Dejarnette's car on a warm day in May. East 68th and Cedar, the lower east side of 1960s Cleveland, Ohio, the area where my life began, was the center of my world. Even though we lived in a poor neighborhood, Mama and Daddy were full of hope for us, especially Mama. Don't let Dr. King or any good lookin smart soundin Black person be on TV for that matter. We would all watch the 6 o'clock news on our little Black and White TV, with the colored plastic over the screen that was supposed to make you think you were watching TV in living color. Back in those days, my brother and I had to come in the house when Daddy got home from work— "Chriiiis, Lehhhnie," Mama would sing in long loud tones to reel us in so we could all eat dinner together: Mama, Daddy, my brother Chris and me.

Me and our old TV around 1962

I learned early that trauma was part of life. One Sunday morning, Mama was combing my hair for church in the hallway. She had run the hot comb through my hair the night before and now she was standing in front of me, taking my bang roller out. All of a sudden, I felt something warm on my foot. I looked down and Lord ha mercy! High off some Decon rat poison that Daddy put down, Big Ben was staggerin slowly across my foot, taking his last few breaths, as I leaped and screamed, "I ain't nevah livin in no ole raggedy apartment buildin like this when I get grown. Big ugly nasty things."

We didn't live in Noah's Ark, but we might as well have. It was so close to me. Kids loved to play around the base of the front of the Ark because it sloped down like a sliding board, but instead of aluminum, the Ark's slope was concrete, the same kind the sidewalk was made of, with a bun-shaped extra layer near the edge to round it off—folks used it as a stoop. Kids ran up and down the concrete slide—playing cowboys and Indians, hand-clapping games, tag and anything else they could get away with before a drunk or their parents ran them off.

The Ark was a huge brick building, with lots of apartments like the projects. But unlike the projects, the Ark's apartments were big. The Ark was at least four stories tall and stretched back about the length of nine Cadillacs, with zig zaggin fire escapes on both sides of the building. Mama didn't want us playing around Noah's Ark. She said it was too dangerous. I had a friend, Loria, who lived on the Ark's top floor with her grandma. Mama let me go over Loria's sometimes so I got to see what the inside of the Ark looked like. Just inside of the huge, heavy, heavy metal double doors were about five rows of black mailboxes, the kind with little key locks on them. The walls were glossy dark pink and the ceilings were cathedral-like, with cobwebs here and there. There were no windows in the dimly lit halls, with plenty of blown light bulb sockets. The hall floors were made of long dark brown varnished planks that showed wear and tear from Lysol, Pine Sol, urine and years of traffic. Somebody tried to keep the Ark clean but it never lasted. There was always a hint of urine and trash strewn here and there. The stairs leading to the top of the Ark seemed never-ending, though the landings were few. I never walked down the stairs that led to what I imagined to be a creepy basement filled with dead bodies. But the Ark was full of life, death, hummin radios, thumpin stereos, hearty laughter, loud voices, dirty diaper and garbage smells, mixed with pot, pan, and barbeque grill aromas.

I guess people called it Noah's Ark because so many of God's creations could be found inside: winos, holy rollers, gay folks, couples, singles, families, "regla" folks—young, old, kids, teenagers. Everybody knew everybody. Even if you didn't necessarily consider a person a friend, you knew where they lived and the family they came from. A lot of people were from down south, Alabama, Georgia, Mississippi, Tennessee, South Carolina. Most of them were church-goin folk who worked every day or every day that they could. Some were alcoholics who worked every day and got drunk as often as they could. Some didn't drink, go to church, nor work.

Daddy was our building's acting super. I say acting because we never got a break on rent or anything. He just liked to see it clean. Every month when the landlord came to collect his rent, Mama and Daddy would cuss him out fiercely tag team style. His name was Mr. Moe, a Jewish guy who lived out in Pepper Pike, a suburb of Cleveland. We called all suburbs "White Man's Land." Daddy would always remind Mr. Moe, "You wouldn't negleck yo property out in Pepper Pike like dis." Daddy fixed things around the building and kept the hallway swept and mopped with Lysol since our hallway doubled as a bathroom for boys and men off the street. Daddy always kept the two little patches of dirt in front of the building free of trash, too.

I tried to grow grass out there two or three times. Daddy would help me till the ground and put the seeds down, and tie white twine around four stakes. By morning it would all be torn down. No grass could grow there. Hardly anything or anyone could grow there without being torn down.

Yeah, God made us all different, from different parts of the world etcetera etcetera, but nobody likes being different when you're a kid. We were the only Jamaicans around. And it was all funny talk and funny smellin food to my friends. "Why y'all food smell funny?" "Why yo mutha talk funny?" "Yo mama from Puerto Rico?" Put that together with my parents being older and those were two automatic strikes against me.

I was a daddy's girl-spoiled rotten to the core. Daddy never beat me when I did something wrong. He just preached. Mama did all the beating. Sometimes he would beg her off of me. I was a hardheaded child. I got my butt whupped almost every day.

I knew what time Daddy was supposed to get off the bus from work, and I would keep an eye out, so that when he got off, I'd be right there to greet him. He would scoop me up, twirl me around, and give me a big hug. If he didn't already have a Baby Ruth, a Snicker's, or a Payday in his pocket for me, we'd stop in Mr. Frank's corner store. If I had a friend with me, I'd sing in ascending tones, hitting my highest note on the last word, "Da-dee can *you* buy my friend one, *too*?" And because he loved me so much, he never turned me down.

I used to be pretty good in elementary and junior high, until my interest in being liked by boys overpowered my interest in school. Although Mama stressed to us that we were not better than anybody, she only wanted us to associate with certain kids. Mama sized up folks quick. If they didn't have manners or if they didn't speak "PropaHenglish," Mama didn't want me around them.

I always had two sets of friends. I'm a people person. I had a list of approved friends I could hang with, although I still found a way to be around "jagabats," Mama's word for no account, low-life people. Godzilla could be my friend, as long as he treated me right. One of my best approved friends was Natalie Adams. She lived right across the street from Noah's Ark. Her skin was clear and light. She had long flowing hair. She spoke "PropaHenglish"—a really nice girl. She was a little on the shy side. Extra super smart in school. Her parents had an approved friends' list too, and I was on it. I was probably the *only* one on their list. Natalie and I walked to and from school together every day. If we played together, I had to sit on her porch, or go in her house. She could never leave her yard.

Some of my friends and kids at school hated Natalie because she was "light-skinded," she was the teacher's pet, and she hardly talked to anyone. Some girls used to taunt her, pull her hair and chase her home from school. I was her self-appointed bodyguard, always backing people up off of her, asking them to leave her alone, and explaining to them that she was nice. Jackie Sims would yell, "Natalie, you ain't bedda dan nobody, ya high yellah bitch!" "Leave her alone, she alright," I'd say. The boys loved and worshipped her for her long hair and light skin. They pulled her hair and chased us home, too, but they were chasing Natalie for a kiss, which they never got even if they caught us. She would cry and beg them to leave her alone. I would beg for her too.

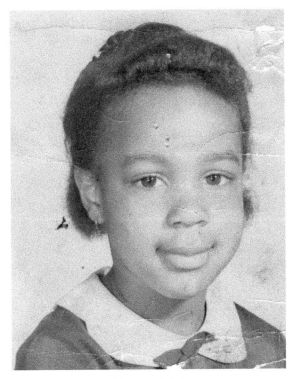
Me around 1966

Now around this time, my big brother Chris and I were best friends. I loved the ground he walked on. One time before I started school, I remember going to the school with Mama and we saw him sitting handsomely among his classmates. Chris was probably in second or third grade. I dashed into his classroom, threw my arms around his neck, and gave him the biggest kiss on the cheek. "Yuck!" he drawled and wiped his cheek with full force.

I learned a whole bunch about being a girl from my brother and his friends. Especially when we were pre-teens, Mama had to work or do things sometimes and she couldn't let me play unsupervised in the neighborhood and she couldn't pay folks to watch me all the time. So, Mama made my brother, Chris, take me everywhere he went. He hated it, but I loved it. I remember leafing through magazines and watching television with my brother and his boys. "Thass me right dere," my brother would say, pointing to some male heroic character, or sports figure. I would point to a similar image and say, "Thass me right dere." And somebody would say, "That ain't none uh you. You a girl. That cain't be you." Or, sometimes my brother and I would be watching television and he'd show me who all the pretty ladies were. Everytime someone came on TV that had long flowing hair or lightskin, he'd say, "she pretty." He would always say, "She ugly" for Black ladies with short natural hair, thick lips, or other African features. If a lady was dark skinned, her hair had to be flowing and her lips couldn't be thick for her to get a "she pretty." My brother didn't realize that that meant that I was ugly. But I did.

I learned how to play baseball and football really well, "for a girl." I was often reminded that being a girl was a handicap by the way the neighborhood boys treated me. When they chose teams, it always came down to me and this tall skinny boy. The captain, who had first dibbs on the last players, would always say "Man, gimme Elaine," in a grudging tone that suggested he was choosing between the devil and the deep blue sea. That was a diss to me, since as a girl, I was one step above "a sissy boy." It was waaaay more of a diss to the tall skinny boy no one wanted. I was always glad they chose me over him. No equality, nowhere in sight. It was already expected that I was not good enough to play with the boys. But I wanted to figure out how to make them like me. How should I act? I tried really hard to be good at sports. I even wished I was a boy.

My tomboyishness almost got knocked out of me one day while playing catcher for a baseball game. A boy "lost control" of his bat and knocked me almost senseless to the ground. I had a huge knot on my forehead and pain unspeakable. I sobbed out of control and my brother was mad at me. "Thass what you git. I told Mama you don't need to be playin wit us no way. Come on!" He grabbed my hand and led me home. I was mad at my brother for that 'cause I always felt that the batter hit me in my head on purpose.

We were a close-knit family. Before Mama had two jobs—the school on second shift and dayswork in the daytime—we all ate dinner together, sometimes breakfast too. My brother and I could play outside until the street lights came on, when we had to come in and get our baths and get our clothes ready for school.

We all went to Holy Grove Baptist church together every Sunday. That's when I fell helplessly in love with good singing. Her name was Gene Gates. That sista had a special voice! When she opened her mouth and let the voice flow, folks fell to the floor, cried, shouted and knew that God was real. And, it was life changing to experience the Mother of the Church get the Holy Ghost. I don't know how her hands took it. She had the loudest and best soul claps of anyone in the world. All ushers, deacons and nurses hovered near her every Sunday cause she would turn a church out! I loved that church. I got my first singing lessons in the junior choir:

> We're marching
> We're marching up to Zion
> That beautiful city of God
> We're marching
> We're marching up to Zion
> Beautiful city of God

AND

We are soldiers

We're in the army

We have to fight although we have to cry

We have to hold up the blood-stained banner

We have to hold it up until we die

AND

Blessed assurance

Jesus is mine

Songs like that were burned onto the template of my mind. Little did I know that later in life I'd be singing those songs in places as far away from church as Lucifer is from God. I loved being in the junior choir. Our director heard my voice and began giving me lead parts. The nurses, mother's board and deacons always encouraged me: "Take yo time chile," "Let the Lord use you," and "That's alright." We went to Sunday school, studied our lessons, and prayed at night at our bedsides and before dinner at the dining table. On Saturday nights Mama gave us Bible studies: The Ten Commandments, John 3:16, The Psalms.

Psalm I: Blessed is the man that walketh not in the counsel of the ungodly, nor standeth in the way of sinners, nor sitteth in the seat of the scornful. But his delight is in the law of the Lord; and in his law doth he meditate day and night.

And we would pray: *Our Father which art in Heaven, Hallowed be thy name…*

I remember being happy, feeling loved and good about myself, even though we had roaches, an occasional rat, even though the boys always picked me last for their teams, and no guys chased me for kisses. But something happened that really rocked my world. I never knew until I was an adult, after I had my children and was recovering from drinks, drugs and the streets how much this affected me.

One evening Mama took Chris to a cub scout meeting.

"Gilly, see dinnah on the stove for you and Lainey. We'll be home latah, hear?" Daddy seemed alright. I was happy. Mama and Chris left and Daddy and I ate our dinner. Pretty soon Daddy started complaining about everything.

"Yo mammy is the best I ever seen. Look how she got all dis mess packed up ovuh dis broom closet. If it wasn't for me she uh still be in a shack in Jamaica."

For some reason, Daddy was grumbling and mumbling. I don't know what was wrong. Maybe Mama and Chris came home too late. Maybe Daddy was just jealous. I know he didn't like it that she worked. I wanted to stay awake until Mama and Chris came back from the meeting, but I fell asleep.

"Rassclot!" "Son of bitch!"

"You no good bitch!"

"You is a *no* good Muddafuckahhhh!"

Crash! Boom! Thud!

I jumped up, swung open my bedroom door to Daddy and Mama looking strange. Mama had flung a pot of boiling hot dogs onto Daddy's chest, some of which splashed back onto her own. Mama was holding a rag to her head. Daddy had bust Mama in the head with a ketchup bottle. Blood was everywhere. I just screamed, cried, shook, and screamed, cried and shook until my voice was gone. Mama tried to quiet me down, but nothing could comfort me. My brother was also shaken to the core. He was talking to Mama and Daddy, trying to get them to stop the fussin and fightin. I was too busy crying to know if my brother cried too.

Mrs. Walcott came and banged on the door. Somebody let her in. Mama told her to take us downstairs until the police came. I never saw them when they got there. I just know that somehow I went to school later that morning and I couldn't settle down, crying and sobbing off and on, until the school called Mama and told her to pick me up, that something was wrong with me. I don't remember who took me home. All I know is when I got back there, I hated everybody. I didn't want nobody to say nothing to me. I hated all of them. Something was wrong with them. I didn't feel right and I just knew that none of us loved each other. From that night on, Mama and Daddy never slept together again. From that night on, Mama and I shared a bedroom. Daddy had his own room. That was the only fight they ever had, though it lasted all of our lives. And we just lived over it.

•2•

Sights, Sounds, My Wounds/My Womb

One plus one
We havin some fun
In the bedroom
All day and part of the night
Two plus two
What can we do
In the bedroom
All day and part of the night
Three plus three
He said let me see
In the bedroom
All day and part of the night
Four plus four we laid on the floor
In the bedroom
All day and part of the night
Five plus five
He opened it wide
In the bedroom
All day and part of the night
Six plus six

He put in his dick
In the bedroom
All day and part of the night
…
Ten plus ten
We did it again…

68THSTREET WAS TYPICAL of many inner city hoods. On the other end of 68th there was a grocery store that was owned by the same guy that owned one of the local after hour joints, My Pal. Mostly everybody in the neighborhood had at least one bill with him, some had two: one for groceries, the other for liquor.

There seemed to be two things that irked some people: country Negroes and winos. One of my best friends, Jeffrey Williams, was from down south. The guys in the neighborhood called him everything but the chile of God. "Country," "Jethro Bodine," "Jeffro," "Bama," "Cotton comes to Harlem," "Hillbilly," "New Country Cornflakes."

That boy had to fight darn near every day. He let them know, "I might be country, but I ain't no punk."

"Did you see dem country ass niggas barbequing on the front porch?"

"Dat country ass nigga got dem big ass white wall tires, dat funny ass cucaracha horn and got da nerve to have air shocks on that raggedy ass green car. Dat's a country muthafucka right dere."

It's so funny that people teased folks who were fresh from the south, when most all of the Black folks around were only one generation removed from the south themselves.

The winos never really bothered anybody. These were the Negroes that everybody pointed to as the Negroes you didn't want to become. Those that couldn't hold down a job just hung around the place. Shell shocked veterans of foreign wars. Vietnam vets. Young dudes who leaned on the corner light posts to add to the décor of the hood, beggin for change, drinkin Mad Dog and Wild Irish Rose. Some of them laid themselves down on the ground in front of My Pal's store. Others hung around the store impatiently waiting for My Pal so they could get their top of the morning shorty (smallest bottle of wine you can buy). Sometimes boys would throw rocks at them to get them out of the street. Some of these guys lived in Noah's Ark and some were cool like Grover, Booty Green, and Pete. They were my personal favorites.

"Good morning, young lady."

"Good morning, Mr. Grover," I would say on my way to pick up Natalie for school in the morning. Mr. Grover loved to sing Rufus Thomas' hit song once he got his wine in him:

I gotcha, uh huh huh

You thought I didn't see you nah didn't you, uh huh huh

You tried to sneak pass me nah didn't you, uh huh huh

He sounded just like Rufus Thomas' record, too. Popping out his big dead fish eyes, Mr. Grover's voice rang out like thunder. Sometimes he would sneak up behind me and gravel out that song. That would make me pee my pants!

I was chubby with large lips. So, kids called me Weep Wow (spoken in a Louie Armstrong drawl to emphasize my thickness). Weep Wow was a sound effect that was played on the Little Rascals every time Chubsy Wubsy appeared. Other names people called me were chub, fat girl, liver lips, rubber lips and bubble lips. There was one kid called Dead Eye, Knot Eye, Knot, and What

Knot, on account of a large lump near one of his eyes. Another girl had spots on her legs in the aftermath of the chicken pox. Her nickname was Spotty Dotty. Planet of the Apes was the nickname of one of the neighborhood boys—you know why. No difference or identification marker was left unspoken.

We played Jacks, Jump rope, Hide and Go Seek:

Last night, night before

24 robbers at my door

I got up

let em in

Hit em in the head wit a rollin pin

Are you ready?

We played Hide and Go Git It, It, Dodge Ball, Hopscotch, told scary stories. The scariest to me was the Neckit Man. Somebody always saw a man with no clothes on rubbing his "thing," chasing kids in somebody's back yard late at night.

We played hand clapping games:

Mama's in the kitchen burning that rice,

Daddy's on the corner shootin that dice,

Brother's in jail raisin up hell,

Sister's on the corner sellin fruit cocktail.

Rockin Robin...

AND

I'm a cool cool girl

From a cool cool town

It take a cool cool boy to cool me down

And if you don't like my apples

Don't shake my tree

And if you don't like my Uhm

don't mess wit me

Kiss my acka backa

My soda cracker

My gto

My booty hole

My jelly bean

My gangsta lean

My submarine

We had body movements and steps that went with the rhythm to the words of the rhymes. Too much fun-uh-un!

And Casshius Clay didn't have nothing on the crap shooting Negroes in my hood:

"Baby need a new pair of shoes." "Betchu 'ont barg." "I'ma make dis 4 for Lil Joe from Cocamoe." "See 6 or 7 bound, if you can't swim yo ass gone drown."

Everybody always got new outfits for the 4th of July, Easter and Christmas. It didn't matter that they came from what must have been the cheapest store next to the thrift shop—Giant Tigers. You would have thought that Black folks were equal if you saw how we dressed, cooked, and celebrated for Independence Day. Same with Thankstaking. I never heard of Juneteenth until I started taking Black Studies courses at Cleveland State University. I don't think any of our teachers knew anything about it either. For the record, Juneteenth is an African American holiday that celebrates our freedom. All manner of evil conspired to withhold the fact of freedom from the enslaved people in Texas until June 19th, 1865, although The Emancipation Proclamation declared us free January 1, 1863.

One thing about the adults in the neighborhood, somebody would always be on their porch if it wasn't cold out. And you couldn't walk pass people without speaking to them. Miss Purline would say, "Did I sleep witchu last night?"

"No, ma'am"

"Well, what about dog kiss my foot? You 'on't be walkin pass nobody widout speakin."

"Hi Miss Purline, Hi Miss Stanley, Hi Miss Costella, Good morning Miss Johnson."

If one of those old ladies saw you doing something, you could be sure that they'd tell on you. And they would tell you, "I'ma tell yo mama on you. You betta git on home." And, if one of them old biddies was working my nerves, I wouldn't let them know it. Mama would beat the living daylights out of me.

During elementary, I was a good kid. I played violin in the orchestra, sang in the choir, I was in the smart kids' reading group. I was outgoing. I was right up there under Natalie Adams in class rank.

By the time I got to junior high school, Natalie had moved away. And another thing changed—my body. My chubby pounds disappeared, leaving me with a nice butt, (an African feature that Black people have not been taught to hate... yet), and small but erect breasts, that a lot of men made me feel self-conscious about. I used to hate to walk down Cedar Avenue to the store.

"Honk, Honk!" These nasty old men, white and Black would blow at me. Some of them would yell out of their windows.

"Hey babe"—looking at me like they could see through my clothes.

"Say it to ya mama"! I'd yell back, like I'd heard other girls do, even though Mama always told me not to talk to strangers.

I began hanging out with several adventurous neighborhood girlfriends, most of them not on Mama's approved list: Josephine, Nay Nay, Little Bitty, Marsha, Pat and Elizabeth. Little Bitty was my favorite. That girl could down a Colt 45 just as quick as a ice cold glass of water on a scorching hot summer's day. Bitty was real short, a cute little dark brown thing. She wore her hair in a natural.

Had the prettiest little face, straightest white teeth and nicest smile of anyone I knew. To be 14 years old, that girl's breasts seemed waaay too large! But they were all hers, all natural. She enjoyed a high degree of success among a few boys in the neighborhood. She had moved onto E. 68th St from down south. She smoked weed and had sex. I hadn't done any of those things...yet.

Bitty's mother was a divorced single parent and worked during the day. Their apartment was perfect for playing hooky, since most of the grown ups that lived in her building were away during the day. My girl Josephine "found" a large sum of her mother's boyfriend's money hidden in a chest of drawers in her mother's bedroom. Thus began my school cuttin career. Josephine had loads of money and we needed to cut school so we could have time and opportunity to enjoy it all.

Josephine bought us cigarettes, weed, beer, McDonald's, and candy. Some of the girls even bought clothes with Josephine's mother's boyfriend's money. I knew I couldn't take anything that Mama didn't buy into our house, so I just ate the food, snacks, smoked a little weed and some cigarettes and drank a little beer. I wasn't really into gettin high at that point in time.

Little Bitty began to invite boys to join our school-cuttin parties at her house. These boys were older than us— 17 and older—and they weren't from the neighborhood. I don't even know how she met them. I was probably 12 and a half and was barely in the 7th grade.

No boys had really shown any interest in me up until this point. I mean I had a boy that tried to look up my dress once in elementary school, but that was about the extent of it. When we played Hide and Go Git It, nobody ever tried to git me. All the guys in elementary were in love with Natalie Adams—B.B. Evans, Harold Diggins, Aaron Burns, Tyrone Smith. Little Bitty began going with this dude named Wilbur. He had a brother, Rat, that she set me up with. Rat and I talked on the phone once to confirm that we would be at Bitty's on an agreed date.

I was so excited. *What should I wear? Will he think I'm special and pretty? Will he fall head over heels in love with me?* I couldn't wait to know what a real date felt like. The biggest day of my life finally came! There were several boys in the house that day. Girls and guys began to couple off into different bedrooms.

"Hey girl," Rat said in a deceptively seductive playful tone.

"Hello," I sang in my best sweet girly falsetto.

Rat offered his hand to me to escort me from the living room couch to the bedroom. I gave him my hand to be led away sheepishly.

I can't let Rat know I'm a virgin, I thought. I would just pretend that I was grown and sexy.

He kissed me on the lips, stuck his tongue in my mouth. No sparks flew.

This is not all that good. But maybe it will get better, I thought.

He began to move his weight on me, to push me back onto the bed. *Okay, he wants to get on top of me.* Next thing I knew, he *was* on top of me. He pulled my pants and panties down, sayin, "Girl I ain't gonna put it in" as he tried desperately to get it in. It wouldn't go. I cried and wiggled out of the way of his thing, but that made him hump faster and harder and sweat on me more. I felt something squirt out into the opening of my vagina. As soon as he was done, he jumped up off of me.

"Girl, why you so tight?" He grinned. "Hurry up and let's get out of this hot ass room," he chuckled. I took a napkin off the dresser, wiped myself, straightened up my clothes, and followed him out of the room. As he walked out, he slapped five with a couple of his boys and sniggered, right in front of my face. "Man, that shit was so tight, I had to use some Vaseline." As I approached the bathroom, he started talking to my girl Nay Nay, trying to get her to go into the bedroom with him next. I sat on the toilet thinking, "Sex is awful and pointless and my coochie hurts." I got off the toilet, wet some tissue paper with some cool water and tried to nurse myself.

As I walked out the bathroom, Rat and Nay Nay were nearby talking. Whatever he was saying to her made her all full of smiles and purrs. "You Elaine's boyfriend. I can't do that." Little Bitty would come back and tell me stuff that Nay Nay and Rat did or said. I felt stupid. I never cut school with them again after the Rat episode.

I started getting sick in the mornings. If I smelled bacon frying, I would throw up. If I ate breakfast, I would throw up. If I woke up, I would throw up! My stomach started gettin big, too. "Damn, I'm pregnant." I drank some Clorox one day hoping that that would make it go away, but it only made me sick. I needed to see my period, but it wouldn't come for nothing. I had only had one period before, so I was still hoping that maybe it was just clogged up inside me some kinda way.

That was my first horrible summer in Jamaica, too. Every summer, I loved going to Jamaica. I loved to see the goats, the chickens, pick bananas, mangoes, pineapples off the trees in my Grandma's backyard, eat mangoes, drink coconut water and be spoiled rotten by my Grandma:

Po ting, live a farin

Don't ave nobody ovuh dey

Fadda God keep mi granpickni dem

My little cousin Billy knew I was sick. He came to my bedside one morning, brought me a pretty flower, and sang a song to me:

Tek back my flowah and give mi Elaine.

Tek back my flowah and give mi Elaine.

Tek back my flowah and give mi Elaine.

The sweeter he sang it, the more I cried. I was scared and depressed. Oh Lord. I was "the lucky one" who got to grow up in the U.S. and my family was proud of that. The U.S. is the land of oppachunity. One of my uncles wanted to show me off to his high class in-laws.

"This is my American niece, Elaine," bragged Uncle Brownie to his Father in-law. "Lainie, say hello to Mr. Campbell."

"Hello Mis...ter Camp...bell" I said in shaky measured syllables as I swallowed down the vomit that slowly crept up from my stomach. Just as I was going to shake Mr. Campbell's hand, the bad feeling came over me suddenly, no time to get to the outhouse. The vomit erupted out of my mouth and I blahhed! All over the Campbell's nice shiny tile floor. I could tell that Uncle hated my guts. I did too.

"You don't know when you feel sick, ee?" He glared.

"I'm sorry, Uncle."

That is all I could say. What could I do? I was a living embarrassment.

When we got back from Jamaica, I told Bitty. She told Nay Nay and pretty soon it got back to Mama. She asked me, if I wanted the baby and who was the father. I was scared and ashamed of myself. I couldn't tell her that I had sex. I couldn't tell her that I was raped on my first "date." I couldn't tell her that the guy's name was Rat. I probably should have told her something before we went to Jamaica. But I kept hoping the baby would go away by itself. Now, Mama had to dig up every dime she had. I couldn't tell her the truth. Rat didn't like me and he sure wasn't gon' want the baby.

Little Bitty told Rat I was pregnant. He said, "It ain't none of mines"—a refrain that I would hear at least 3 more times over my lifetime with subsequent pregnancies. I begged Mama.

"Please help me Mama," I cried.

"I don't want no baby. Mama, I'm sorry. I don't want no baby."

Chzzzzzshzz! Mama sucked her teeth when she was flabbergasted. "Didn't mi tell yuh, yuh nuh ready fi sex, a grown people business. Let me see yuh belly." She lifted up my blouse and felt my stomach. Chzzzzzshzz! Yuh gone far. Look how you mash up yuhself." Chzzzzshzz! Mama lit a cigarette, took a long drag, blew it out briskly, as she paced back and forth a couple times. She made her way over to the phone at our little brown phone stand near the windows of our dining room.

She broke open the Yellow Pages and just started calling around to look for someone who would give me an abortion.

We went to a doctor the next day. The doctor confirmed, I was almost five months! No go. He referred us to another doctor, who referred us to another doctor in Queens, New York, who agreed to perform the abortion. I was too far gone for doctors in my state. I remember they put a big long needle in my stomach, in a little while, my belly began to ache really bad. A nurse came and held my hand. Then others came and got the baby out of me. I never saw anything. I didn't want to.

I knew I killed somebody. Somebody who didn't deserve to be killed. Somebody who probably would have been a nice person, if I had given it a chance. But I was 13. I didn't think I could handle having a baby. I just couldn't even think about it.

I think Mama had insurance, but I never went to any kind of counseling to find out how that abortion affected me. I didn't want to talk about it, but everyone else in the community did. Everywhere I went, I could see people pointing, whispering and staring. And even if they didn't, I felt like they did. I was an outlaw. Whatever self-esteem I had died with the rape and the baby.

Dear God, I'm sorry. Forgive me for my sins. I killed somebody, God. I didn't mean to do it. I shamed my parents and disobeyed them. Give me another chance to show you that I am a good girl. Don't send me to hell. God, if you forgive me for this, I'll be good and I won't get in no more trouble. I promise.

I would lay in my bed every night, pray and read the Ten Commandments over and over. I'd write:

Thou shalt not kill. Honour thy mother and thy father that thy days may be long upon the land which the Lord thy God giveth thee.

I killed somebody. I dishonored my father and my mother. I lied.

I met Andrew Ball through Josephine and her boyfriend, Greg. Andrew's mother lived in the King Kennedy projects around the corner from Little Bitty, who had moved away from E 68th St. Andrew didn't live in the projects with his mom. His parents broke up when he was a little boy and he grew up with his father—and the bad boys' homes of Ohio. Little did I know that Andrew had been in damn near all of them, in and out from a very early age: Juvenile Detention Center aka JDC, Boys' Industrial School (aka BIS), Hudson Farm, Maumee. You name it, he had Been There and

Done That. When Andrew's mother was a 15 year-old girl down in Chattanooga, Tennessee, her father gave her to Andrew's father, Mr. Ball, a much older man, who would become her husband. This was common back in the day down South. Mr. Ball proceeded to pump 6 boys into Mrs. Ball, drink, gamble and treat Mrs. Ball badly. She found her way out of that marriage. Eventually, she remarried, had 4 more kids for her new husband and that's who she lived with in the projects around the corner from Josephine's boyfriend, Greg.

Even though Mrs. Ball was remarried and had a new name, everyone still called her "Miss Ball." When Little Bitty moved into the projects, Josephine started hangin over there a lot. That's how she met Greg, who lived one flight down from Bitty. From the time they hooked up, Josephine and Greg were inseparable. Josephine began almost living at Greg's house, so I started visiting her over there.

One day, we're sitting there outside the building, chillin, when this tall, slim, good-looking, caramel complexioned brotha pulls up and jumps out of a bright green Oldsmobile. He walks over greets us all and pulls Greg over to the side as Greg proceeds to excuse them a few feet out of our earshot for a few moments. Walking towards Andrew's car, Greg called over to Josephine, in a loud voice:

"Hey we'uh be back in a few. We gotta make a run."

"Cool, but y'all betta be comin back before it git too late cause we need a ride home. We gotta go to school tomorrow," she replied.

Neither Greg nor Andrew went to school. Andrew was 17 and Greg was 19. Josephine was 15 and I was 13. When they came back they had wine, beer, weed, cigarettes, and food. They seemed to be much more cheerful.

Andrew suggested, "Hey, let's ride aroun a little before we drop y'all off."

Josephine looks at me. I look at God's gift to humanity and the answer was:

"*Yeah!*"

"Hey sexy, why on't chu ride up here wit me in da front," Andrew said, as he lit up his joint and passed it to me. I signaled to him to pass it on to the back, as I scooted happily into the front seat.

"Oh, you on't smoke?" He asked.

"Not that much," I said.

"You a good girl. I like dat. What's yo name? Where you live at?"

"Elaine—sixty eif (68th) and Cedah," I said in the softest sexiest voice I could muster. "What's yo name and where do *you* live?" I said trying to hold up my end of the conversation.

All the time, in my mind, I know he must have already run a background check on me through his boy, Greg. My problem was, I didn't run one on him.

"Andrew——83rd and Chester," he said, as he looked through the rear view mirror and noticed that Josephine and Greg were hoggin his joint:

"Would y'all good people min' passin that J back up here?"

We cruised through Edgewater Park area. Came back across St. Clair, Superior and on over around through Hough. It was starting to get late and I didn't want my parents to be angry with me for breaking curfew, which was 9:00 p.m. I was trying really hard not to mess up again. I had already put them through enough.

"Hey y'all I gotta go home," I said just above a whisper.

Andrew looked me up and down.

"You gotta man?"

"No," I answered.

"Can I see you again tomorrow? Want me to pick you up from school? What school you go to?" Andrew questioned.

"East Tech, but you cain't pick me up from there. My mother work there and somebody might see me," I said lying through my teeth.

I actually went to Central Jr. High and that's where Mama worked, but I didn't want Andrew to know that I was 13. He seemed so grown up and he was so cute. I was so happy that he was interested in me. He was actually the first guy that seemed to like me and I didn't want to jeopardize that.

"Hey Andrew," said Josephine, "Drop us off close to the corner of our street."

I was glad that she didn't want her mother and her mother's boyfriend to see her getting out of a car either.

"Girl, meet me right here tomorrow at fo thirty. Don't ha' me sittin out here fa nothing," Andrew said in a half joking voice.

"I won't," I said, opening the car door.

Both Josephine and I hopped out of the car not far from the corner and rushed toward our doors, as we exchanged see you tomorrows.

That night I could hardly sleep. I wanted tomorrow to come quick, fast and in a hurry.

Next day, I put on the best pair of jeans I owned, a lotta lipstick, eye make-up, and mascara. I must have looked like a fool, because Mama told me I needed to go wash that mess off of my face.

"Aww, Mama all the girls at school be wearin make-up like this. Ain't nothing wrong wit it."

"Tek di heap a mek-up aff. You nuh need it," she demanded.

"Chzzzzsss," I sucked my teeth and stomped back into the bathroom to wash it off.

"You want I give yu someting fi stomp fuh, huh?"

"Nah, Mama," I said as I turned the faucet on and began washing off the layers.

"Bye Mama," I said as I blasted out of the bathroom, down the hall and out the front door. "Study yuh lesson," Mama yelled after me.

I wasn't studyin nothin that day cept Andrew Ball. I couldn't wait until 4:30! He was parked right near where he had dropped us off the night before. When he saw me comin', he pushed open the passenger's side door.

"Hey sexy, how you doin?"

I loved it when he said that to me. "I'm alright," I sang.

We cruised around the city, as he interviewed me, basically, for the position of his "main woman."

"So you ain't got no man, huh?"

"I told you no, yesterday. You ain't got no woman?"

"Naw, *you* gone be my woman... If you meet the qualifications," he said like he was God's gift to womanity. He was older and wiser than boys my age. He had his own car. Plus, he was cute as hell, and he thought I was cute. He met all of my foolish criteria. We drove along full speed ahead.

Andrew was a daredevil. He lit up a joint, took a couple big drags and passed it to me. I said, "Naw, I uh take one a dem Kools doe." He passed me his pack of Kools. I took one out and fired it up. I had to smoke something to fit in.

"Would you do anythang to help yo man?"

"Yeah, if we loved each other," I said.

"Cause half a dese girls out here claimin dey women, ain't really down. A woman dat's really down for her man is hard to come by dese days out here. It's a bunch a girls out here perpetrating the fraud. Is you a woman or a girl?"

"I'ma woman."

"Well, I'ma hafta put you on probation to see if you really down."

"Okay," I said.

Andrew pulled into a driveway near 83rd and Chester.

"Come on sexy, get out. We goin in."

There was a dark-skinned brother working on some cars in the backyard, wearing gray overhauls. Andrew grabbed me by the hand as we walked toward him.

"Hey Dave, come over here and meet my new woman, Elaine."

As David approached, Andrew whispered to me that David was Greg's sister's babyfather.

"Boy, this fine young thang ain't none a yo woman," David chuckled as he flashed a set of beautiful sparkling white teeth.

"How you doin baby?" he said as he stretched out his hand for me to shake.

David was a handsome young man, with deep dimples and a soft-looking wooly afro. David and his father lived on the first floor of this massive three-family house. Andrew and a couple of his brothers lived on the 3rd floor, the rest of his brothers and their father lived on the 2nd floor.

Andrew and I proceeded to go upstairs to the third floor. He unlocked his bedroom door: "This is my spot."

"Oh, it is your spot okay. I see all of your clothes."

There was a small black and white TV, a very wide bed and a lot of clothes, kinda strewn around to one side of the bed and in between a big old antique looking brown dresser. I tried not to notice the sheets that were placed over the curtain rods up to the three big windows that overlooked the house and that faced East 83rd Street.

"Well ain't you gon' sit down?" he asked.

"Yeah," I said as I sat down on the bed.

I'm sure I looked awkward because I sure felt awkward, just sitting there not knowing what to say and definitely not wanting him to ask me for sex. I had just had an abortion earlier that year and was still trying to keep my promise to God. Andrew turned the TV and radio on with the volume of the radio up and the TV down low.

"My oldest brotha got his shit togetha. He drive a truck, plus he hustle on the side. He got a wife and two little girls. They got a nice house, a nice ride. When him and his broad go out, they be sharp as a mutha. That nigga livin. That's how me and you gon' be. All a nigga gotta do is get some bank and everything else'uh fall in place. You know what Ahm saying?"

He liked to look into my eyes when he talked to me. I liked that a lot. It was like he really wanted to be with me. He was confiding in me. Telling me his dreams. His whole conversation was opening new worlds to me. When he talked to me, I wasn't the girl that got laughed at. I wasn't the fast girl that everybody mumbled and whispered about. I was a woman who understood big things.

"Uhm hmm."

He leaned over and kissed me on the forehead, "Girl, you sho is fine."

I'm thinking, "You is too." But I'm too afraid to say it. The next thing I know, he's all over me, kissing me, searching out my body with his hands, and sticking his tongue in my mouth. It felt good. Boom, Boom Boom! Somebody knocked on his door.

"Who is it?" Andrew asked.

"Man, open this muthafuckin do' if you want cho money nigga or else don't ask me fa shit latah."

I jumped up to straighten up my hair as Andrew made his way to the door. It was his brother, Wayne. Wayne pulled out a wad of cash and peeled off some bills slappin them into Andrew's hand, braggin,

"That's what I'm talkin bout." Wayne was a shorter and darker version of Andrew, just as handsome.

"And, who is this lovely lady?"

"This Elaine, Elaine this my brother Wayne. We call him Lil T."

"Hi," I said. Lil T eyed me up and down and said,

"Boy, you don't know what to do with a sweet young thang like that."

"Nigga mind yo business."

"Oh you can bet I'ma do that nigga. That's why I keep these green backs, witcha broke ass."

"Don't you see I got company."

"Take care, Elaine. I hope I see you again."

"Nigga, if you do see her, she'll be wit me. She mine. Goodnite," Andrew said as he slammed the door.

Little did I know that Andrew and Lil T were two of the thieving-est Negroes on God's green earth. They could steal the sugar out of Kool-Aid.

After Lil T left, we were alone again. We lay in his bed for what seemed like a short time, smoking cigarettes and talking. Andrew looked into my eyes and told me all about the desires of his heart. I hardly said a word about my goals or dreams. I just soaked in all of his. Suddenly, I said "What time is it?" My mother worked night shift and it was way past time when she would have been home from work.

"I gotta get home. Can you take me?"

"Okay."

We straightened ourselves up and made our way back to his car.

All I could think about on the ride home was, "Mama gon' kick my ass." The worse part about sneaking in late at my house was that I shared a bed with Mama. She knew exactly what time I crept in. I slid my key in the door, eased my way in, crept downstairs to the basement and found some pajamas to put on. I changed in the basement. That way, I didn't have to fiddle around when I got upstairs. I quietly opened the bedroom door and tippytoed around to my side of the bed moving the covers ever so slowly when Mama holla'd:

"What time it is?"

My heart jumped right up into my throat. "I don't know, Mama."

"Where you was, ee? You went to school today?"

"Yes, Mama, I went to school."

I just knew Mama was gon' kill me, but for some reason, she just let me lay down.

•3•
The Ropes

ANDREW PARKED AT THE END of my street and began driving me to school every day. I had him believing that the reason he was dropping me off at the Junior High instead of the High School was because my first class was at the Junior High but that I actually went to the High School. In retrospect, I think he knew I was lying and didn't care that I was barely 14 years old. We started seeing each other non-stop—before school, after school. At first I was doing okay with curfew, but I began coming home later and later, especially after we did "it."

It happened the first night that he took me to the drive-in. It was me, Andrew and his cousin, Dee. On the way, we stopped on Hough Avenue to buy Andrew's daily supply of "get high." After he came out of the store, he always took some pills, a big swig of Boone's Farm wine, and lit up a joint. We cruised through the city and finally ended up around the corner from the Miles Drive-In. Andrew got out of the car, opened the trunk, signaled to me and Dee, and instructed us:

"Y'all gotta hop in. I'll pop the trunk when it's time for y'all to come back to y'all seats."

Me and Dee hopped in the trunk and in a few minutes, Andrew popped the trunk and we dashed into the car. The movie was *Foxy Brown* starring Pam Grier. I loved Pam Grier as Foxy Brown. She was one of the most beautiful women in the world and everything Andrew wanted in a woman. Foxy Brown wasn't scared of nothing. She was superbad, a super fighter. She went toe to toe with drug dealers in the hood and big time mafia criminals, from the streets to the suites. Foxy would pull a gun out from under her wig and cap a son of a gun. Andrew was in total love with her. All through the movie,

"That's a baad bitch right dere! That's what every nigga in the world need, a baad bitch like dat ridin wit him."

"Damn, you in love wit her or something?"

"Yeah, I do love me some Foxy Brown. You *my* Foxy Brown. How bout dat?"

Now that deserved a huge hug, which I gladly leaned over the arm rest and gave him. What he say that for. That's all I needed to hear. Every time the camera showed Foxy doing her thang I was takin major notes, her stance, her sex appeal. I imagined myself looking like her.

Andrew loved him some Boone's Farm wine, too. Dee only got one or two swigs. But the rest went straight down Andrew's throat during the movie. The empty fifth bottle doubled as Andrew's urinal. I'm telling you, he nearly filled the whole thing up! And he had the nerve to put that bottle on the floor of the back seat.

"Thass nasty!" I said.

"Well, whatchu want me to do? Piss on the ground or th'ow the bottle away when we get back down the way?"

"You coulda went to the bathroom."

"Girl, please."

That was one thing about him. He was a direct and to the point brother—a quality that I still respect.

When we left the drive-in, we drove back to the projects to drop Dee off. As Dee was exiting Andrew's car, one of his boys, Kirtland, jumped in the back seat beggin'.

"Hey man, whatchu got?" he asked as he searched the ashtrays for weed and cigarette butts.

Before we knew anything, he reached down on the floor of the back seat and put the Boone's Farm bottle to his mouth and drunk a big swig of Andrew's urine. Me and Andrew started dying laughing. Kirtland flung open the backseat door and starting gaggin. "Andrew you a dirty muthafucka. Got me in here drankin yo piss!"

"I ain't have you drankin shit, you beggin-ass muthafucka. Teach yo beggin-ass a lesson. Buy yo own supply. Git yo broke-ass outta here" and we pulled off, burning rubber.

"See baby, a nigga like him is a bum. He ain't neva had shit and ain't gone neva have shit. You know why? Cause he ain't got no game. He a lame-ass nigga. A nigga gotta have some hustle about hisself in nis world. You got some game about yo self, I know cause you like a nigga like me. You love yo man?"

"Uhm, hmm."

Next thing I know we were pulling up into his driveway. We went upstairs into his room. Somehow, I knew we were gonna do "it" that night. We had done stuff before but we never went all the way.

We were both lying on the bed and he began to kiss me, and I kissed him back. We kissed each other. His lips were soft and yummy and he was gentle and nothing, I mean nothing, felt wrong. He unbuttoned my blouse first, slowly, button by button. We began breathing together. Our rhythm became one. I was already in total love with him. After all, he made me his "main woman." He undid my bra. I wiggled out, as he lovingly kissed my nowhere near the size of Foxy Brown breasts; yet he made me feel like they were the biggest, best, breasts in this whole world. I unhooked and unzipped my jeans. He took off all of his clothes, as I pulled down mine.

I had never seen a boy totally neckit (naked) in real life. He was beautiful. I wanted to make him happy, so I let him do everything he was doing. Mama put me on birth control pills after the abortion. She stressed to me that I still wasn't ready for sex until I was an adult. but that I should take the pills. At least I didn't have to worry about getting pregnant, if he wanted me to go all the way with him. The problem came in when he began pushing my head down near his thing.

"Oh, Lord," I said as I began to resist. I never did that and I didn't want to.

"Look, if you gon' be my woman, you gotta do everything. You love me don't you?"

"Yeah."

"Well, put it in yo mouf and lick it."

I heard about sucking before and everything I ever heard about it was nasty. This was waay before Silk's number one R&B song, "Let me lick you up and down til you say stop." I had always heard that white people invented oral sex and that it was nasty, so I wasn't feelin it.

He kept trying to lead my head down there.

"Nooooowoh, I don't want to, thass nasty, " I said as my eyes began to tear up.

"What you cryin fah. I thought you was a woman."

"I am but thass nasty."

"Look, ain't nothing that Listerine can't deal wit, plus, if you my woman we gotta do everything."

Tears flowed down my cheeks as he led it into my mouth.

"Just do it real nice and soft," he instructed.

I felt it grow erect. Then he took it out and told me to rub it in between my legs. I felt myself get wet but I didn't know exactly where to rub it to make it feel good.

He told me to sit on it. It hurt a little.

"Damn girl, you sho is a woman down there. Yo last man musta had a log."

"I had a abortion, I told you. I was almost 5 months pregnant and I only did it once befoe."

"Girl please, you think I was born yesterday."

For him to be so worldly, he didn't understand anything that I had been through. I never got a chance to be honored as a virgin. Or, maybe I didn't honor myself. I should have never hung out with girls who knew more than I did. I should have never gone into a room with a boy that was 19 years old. I guess going into a room with a boy means that you want to be fucked. But I didn't know that. I had had an abortion in the second trimester. The baby I would have had was developed. Whatever the size of my vagina, it was the way it was because I had had a dead baby. All he talked about was how huge I was down there. From that day on, one of his nicknames for me was Big Stuff.

At Central Jr. High School, I wasn't Big Stuff, or Sexy. I was Elaine. The girl whose mother was a cleaning lady for the school and whose mother made friends with all of her teachers and always checked up on her. My French teacher was Mrs. Robertson. Je m'appelle Elaine. I had Ms. Wade for Social Studies. I liked learning about the states, geography, learning to read maps of the globe. In Home Economics, Ms. Heinz taught us how to follow recipes—bake cookies and cakes. We learned how to make pancakes, pasta. We also learned how to stitch by hand and sew on a sewing machine, how to cut out patterns. Every girl had to make an A-line skirt and some made whole outfits, which we had to model in a fashion show. For Algebra, I had Mr. Margolis. My most favorite classes were orchestra and music, I had Miss Dobbins and Miss Meyers. We had spring concerts where the orchestra and the choir would perform, allowing us a chance to show off our musical achievement. I played violin and sang in the choir. I was also on the junior varsity cheerleading squad. At this point my double lives were still under control—Elaine, the school girl and Big Stuff, a "down ass chick" in the making.

Since I had to be in the house early, I still didn't know a whole lot about what Andrew did late nights. I knew he hustled, but I didn't know exactly what hustling meant. One day I was over his house and this chick came over. She knocked and knocked and banged and knocked, and he wouldn't answer the door. She began yelling and cussin. "Nigga, come out here and talk to me. I know you gotta bitch up in there witchu." He says to me, "Look, it's Fat Bitch out dere. She a chick dat give me money. I gotta go talk to her. Don't come outta dis room, hear?"

"Okay."

He left and went outside to talk to her. I peeped through the bedroom window. She was a lot older than me. I guess she must have been around 25. She was a chubby woman. She had on a china doll wig, a short skirt, high heels, a low-cut blouse to accentuate her full bosom, and a lot of makeup. She was a big, glamorous, nice-looking woman, an old skool, Mo'Nique-type.

Anyway, she was cussin Andrew out: "I heard bout you and yo young bitch. What she do? She gittin any money out dis muthafucka or you done start babysittin bitches? I ain't got no money to give you to wine and dine no young no-money gittin bitch."

"Bitch, who you thank you talking to. Bitch you on't run nis. Bitch I runs my bidness. Don't make me fuck you up." *Wham!* He smacked her cross the face. She stumbled back and laid right into him. He grabbed her fist and twisted her hand behind her back.

"Stop it, Andrew. My lip bleedin," she cried.

"Shut up bitch, I run nis. You unnastand. Get in da car!" He unlocked and flung open his car door, shoved her inside, slammed the door, and sped off.

If I had the sense I was born with, I woulda left up outta his house right then before he came back and not looked back. But I didn't. I stayed right there, like a little dummy and waited until he came back a couple of hours later.

"Is that yo woman?"

"What you thank?"

"I think y'all must love each other. The way y'all was out there carrying on. Leave me alone, if you already got somebody. I don't wanna be in no mess. I heard what she said too, that you be winin and dinin me with her money and that I don't git no money."

"You my Big Stuff. Don't worry bout Fat Bitch, I got dat undah control. I need you to undastand yo man. Baby, I'ma hustla.

I hustle women and I makes moves. If you gone be wit me, you gotta undastand what a nigga do."

"I don't have to undastand yo woman. You coulda let her stay. Take me home," I said stomping my feet and walking toward the door.

He came up behind me and grabbed me, holding my shoulders unbearably tight. "I don't stand no back talk from no bitch."

"I ain't none of yo bitch. You a bitch." *Wham!* He slapped me cross the face.

"Don't hit me!" I hauled off and punched him in his face as hard as I could. He punched me in the stomach and I fell on the floor. He began kicking me in my back, as I huddled into the fetal position. "Stop, stop!" I cried and screamed until the kicking stopped.

"Hey, what in hell is goin on out deyah," I heard the rickety voice of Mr. Ball yell from his bedroom. "Stop hittin dat girl, Ondie, what's wrong wid you!"

Mr. Ball looked like a 99 year old wrinkled white man, to me. He was bent over and walked with a cane. He hardly ever came out of his bedroom.

"Bitch, don't you ever hit me. See what you made me do. Go wash up."

"Take me home. I'ma call the Po-Leece on you."

"You gon' call what? Da Po-Leece, well tell em nis," he said as he punched me so hard in the eye with his bare knuckles that I saw lightening.

"Aaahhh, Hahaaaaah, Aaahhh, Aaaahhh." I cried and ran into the bathroom to wash up. I locked the bathroom door and looked in the mirror at my face. I didn't know who I was. My face was distorted. My lip was swollen and I had a huge black eye, with blood in it. It was nearly completely closed. I hated myself. All I could do was sob and sob, as I filled up the face bowl with cold water. I stuck my face in the water. My eye was burning and my body ached. I was less than dirt. Why was this happening to me?

"Hey, come outta dere and let me look at choo."

I was quiet. The house was quiet. I didn't hear nothin'. No TV. No radio. Nothing. When I came out of the bathroom, Andrew was sitting on his bed neckit smoking a joint. "Come here, baby," he called to me gently.

"Please take me home. I'm gon' be in trouble. It's late and I'm sick. I have to work on my face so I can go to school tomorrow."

"Take your clothes off and let me look at choo."

"No, please take me home. I won't call the Po-Leece. I just wanna go home, please," I said.

"Look, I'm sorry, baby. You know I luh you," he said as he pulled me over to him and began unbuttoning my blouse. I didn't feel like fighting or talking or anything. I just let him take off my blouse, my pants and my underwear. As tears rolled down my face, he held it, kissed my eye and tried to wipe away my tears. He began kissing and squeezing my breasts and my bruised ribs. I hated myself.

How come this was happening to me? This doesn't happen to the pretty girls on TV and in the movies. This didn't happen to Foxy Brown.

This is happening to me because I'm ugly. I have big lips and nappy hair. There is nothing special about me. The first boy I liked just fucked me. Now my boyfriend is cheating on me with somebody else. Nobody really loves me. I hate my parents for being lames. How come they didn't make me a pretty girl like the ones in the magazines and on TV, like the lightskinned girls with long hair? How come boys don't worship and adore me? How come we live on East 68th Street anyway? The real families on TV don't live in roach- and rat-raggedy houses.

This was what I deserved for being nothing. *Well, Andrew does like me just the way I am*, I thought. *He even loves me. And, he's gonna marry me.* I loved him. *It's me and him against the world. I'm his "bottom woman." I don't care that he has this older chick givin him money.* All these thoughts ran through my brain as he caressed and kissed my broken body.

"I promise I won't hit choo again, hear?"

I couldn't talk. My mouth, my body, my brain. Everything I had hurt. I couldn't even feel his kisses. I was numb. And who was this "I" anyway?

"Let me make you feel betta," he said. "You wanna spend the night with me tonight? Cat got yo tongue? Okay, I'll take you home Miss Cain't Talk."

After he called himself making love to me, he agreed to take me home. He might as well have been doing it to a blow up doll, because I did nothing to help him enjoy it. It made me hate myself more with each hump. He ran a tub of warm water for me after he finished. He put me in the bathtub and bathed me like a little baby. He went and got a towel out of his dresser drawer, dried me off, got some alcohol, peroxide and lotion out of the medicine cabinet and called-himself doctoring on my wounds. He dressed me and he proceeded to lead me out of the house to the car to take me home. He ran his mouth until we got to the corner of my street:

"Hey, I didn't mean to hit you but you cain't be hittin no man. My mama always said anybody hit me, hit em back. Know what uhm sayin? Look here now, you my bottom woman. Don't worry yoself bout Fat Bitch. She cain't take yo place. You number one. Ain't nann bitch in Cleveland can take yo place, but you gotta defend yo title. You got to have a nigga's back and you the only one can give up yo spot. If you mines, you gotta be all the way wit me. You cain't let no bitch take yo spot, and I definitely ain't bout to let nann nigga out here take you from me. Ya dig?"

I was kinda glad that I was going home late because I wanted to ease in the house without anybody noticing my eye. That's all I was thinking about. I just wanted to go home.

I did my usual. Eased in the basement, took my clothes off. Threw on a big T-shirt, tip toed upstairs as slow as I possibly could. We had the creakiest stairs in the world! Mama had the bedroom door open, but the creaks weren't so noticeable because Mama had her radio on. Thank God. Instead of me trying to sneak in the bed with her, I just curled up damn near under the bed on the floor, so a little of the bedspread would cover me. I hardly got any sleep. I cat napped all night, until daybreak. I eased into the bathroom and got my toothbrush, threw a little toothpaste on the back of my hand. Eased downstairs into the basement. Brushed my teeth and washed up ever so quietly in the sink and found myself some clothes.

I was so worried. How was I gonna make it through the day with my face looking like it did? Shit, I need some shades. I know what. I uh call Josephine.

"Jo, you got some shades I can borrow?"

"Yeah, what you need some shades for in November?"

"You gone let me borrow the shades?"

"Yeah. Andrew pickin you up?"

"Prolly."

"Girl, you know Greg got a car now, so he be pickin me up too."

"Good. Meet me at yo door in a minute wit da shades," talking quickly in hushed tones so nobody would hear me. I managed to get out of the house that morning without anyone seeing my face.

I dashed to her front door and gave a gentle knock. She opened the door. I had my face turned to the side so she couldn't see my eye.

"Come on in."

"Naw, I'm in a hurry. Hand me the shades."

"Hold on."

She came back and stepped out on the porch with the shades and her backpack.

"Here."

As I slipped on the shades, she saw my eye.

"Goddamn! That nigga jump on you?"

"It's alright."

"Girl, you gon' see him again? You lettin him take you to school?"

"He prolly out there on the corner."

"Don't go out there."

"It's alright. I gotta go."

"I uh see you at school."

"Thanks."

He was parked at the corner of my street just like clockwork to take me to school. No hugs or kisses. I sat close to the door with my lip poked out.

"Hey Big Stuff."

I didn't say a word.

"Tonight, I'ma show you how I work. I'ma pick you up later. Be ready to roll, Hear?"

I still ain't say nothing.

"Gimme a kiss."

I got out of the car. No kiss. No words. I just got out the car and slammed the door.

School was starting to get in the way of my life. It's hard being an eighth grader and a "bottom woman." Looking at the blackboard is difficult through a black eye and sunglasses. I was an excellent student in Social Studies, but I couldn't concentrate on questions such as "What is citizenship?" and I didn't feel like participating in discussion or reading, or nothing. My assigned seat was in the front of the class, so it was very easy for Mrs. Wade to notice me:

"What is citizenship, Elaine?"

I began leafing through my doodle-filled notes:

Andrew loves Elaine. Elaine loves Andrew.

I finally ran across something that made sense:

"It's when you are a good participant in society."

"Okay, what is a good participant in society, Elaine? Please take off the sunshades in class."

I looked down at my notes and slid the shades off my face.

"Stop leafing through your notes and use your brain."

"When you follow the rules of society," I muttered staring down at my notebook.

"Okay, please remain after class when the bell rings. I'd like to speak to you."

Oh Lord, she saw it. If she didn't, she will now. My classmate, Linda, sitting next to me saw it and flinched. That was a dead give-away. Okay, I uh just say I hit my face against the dresser.

I stared at my notebook until class was finished. She didn't ask me anything else until after class. *Ring!* I slid my shades back on as soon as I heard the bell.

"What's with the shades, Miss Elaine Richardson?" asked Mrs. Wade.

"I had a accident."

"You have not been your usual self lately. Is there anything I can help you with? Let me see your face?"

"Naw, I'm alright."

"Let me see your notebook."

I handed it over to her.

"Young lady, you need to keep it on the ball. You don't have nearly enough notes here. What's going on with you? You are a smart young lady. You let Mrs. Wade know if you need anything. I'm gonna be talking to your mother, too."

"Ok."

As soon as she let me outta that room, I knew I wasn't going to another class that day. Well, I did go to lunch, which was next period. I went through the lunch line. Paid cash for my lunch, which I thought was dumb. All of my friends got their lunches for free because their parents were on food stamps. My lame parents didn't have enough game to figure out how to not pay for something that other people were getting for free. I spotted one of my best school girlfriends, Linda, and I sat next to her and her girl, Cookie.

"What's up, girl?" asked Linda.

"Nuttin, bout to get up outta here after lunch. Today is just a bad day."

"Why you got on dem shades?"

"I had a accident."

"Uhm hmm, I heard you were goin wit a older guy."

"Who told you dat?"

"Let's just put it like dis, word gits around."

"Tell people to keep my name out dey mouf. Hey, if anybody ask bout me, you ain't seen me. I'm gone."

"Suppose your mother come up here asking me?"

"She ain't got no reason to come lookin for me. I'm signed in. I'm just not goin to no moe classes fa today. I'm gone."

"Girl, you gone git yo ass sent up to the Detention Center."

People always talked about the Detention Center, Blossom Hill, Scioto Village, and the Juvenile Home. I was too slick to get sent up. That was for dummies.

"Nah, I'm cool. I'ma see y'all tomorrah."

I just had to get outta there. I knew Mama worked there and that she might check up on me, but I just felt like the whole world knew about my eye. I eased out of one of the side doors of Central Jr. High School, jumped through the open hole in the wire fence, ran down 43rd Street, across Central Avenue, through the Outhwaite projects, until I got to East 55th. Then I walked until I got over to King Kennedy projects. When I got there, I went over Greg's house. I couldn't go over Ms. Ball's. I didn't want her to see my face. I knew Greg's place was cool. No adult supervision. Even if his mom was home, she never came out of her room.

Sure enough, when I got to Greg's Josephine was there. I wanted to ask her anyway, how Linda nem knew about Andrew and me.

"Jo, you don't be goin around telling people about me and Andrew, do you?"

"Nah, girl, why you say dat?"

"Uhm, cause you the only one dat know all my business dat go to Central."

"Girl, I'm yo bes friend. You know I ain't tole nobody nuthin bout you."

"Cool, I need to stay over here til school over. Can I get a ride to sixty eif when you git ready to go home?"

"Yeah, girl."

I basically stayed in the bathroom washing my face with cold water, using alcohol pads, peroxide, anything I could find in Greg's mother's bathroom to doctor on myself until it was time to go home.

Now usually when I got home, Mama was already gone to work, but this particular day. Mama was still home. She was sittin right dere by the door. As soon as I opened it, she asked:

"You went to school todeh?"

"Yes, Mama."

"What you learn?"

"We learned stuff about citizenship and society, and I answered the questions right in Mrs. Wade's class."

That's all I could truthfully say, before I started making up a bunch of a lies about Algebra, English, and Science. The next thing I know, Mama snatched the shades off my face and gave me one good lick across my arm.

"'Ave mercy Gad! Wha hapm to you?"

"Nuthin, Mama. I fell."

"Yuh tink I'ma dyam fool? Who you runnin around wid, eeh? You wan get yo fool ass kill, ee?"

"No Mama."

"Yo ass is on punishment. Miss Wade call here todeh. You not doin yuh lesson dem good and you cut class todeh. Get yoself upstairs. Mi ago ave yo ass put inna Juvenile Home. You tink you can rip and run in and outta dis ouse and run di streets, while me and yuh fadda work to gi you a roof ovah you dyam head and a betta life? Chzzzzzh!"

"No Mama."

"Git outta my sight before mi gi yuh a nex black eye."

I ran upstairs to my room and cried myself to sleep. I didn't go back out that night to meet Andrew.

•4•

Tricked Out

ANDREW KEPT CALLING THE house for me with his special code: two rings, hang up and one ring meant call him at his mother's house. He started calling early the next morning. I didn't answer. Mama did. He hung up on her every time. She knew what was up. So did he. Well, we didn't have a car. Mama or Daddy didn't drive. And, Mama wasn't gonna walk me to school. She just had to trust that I would make it to school. Mama didn't say anything to me. She just watched me get ready for school. I got dressed in a hurry. I wanted to get out of the house because I knew Andrew was gonna be salty. I got out and walked my normal route to school and there he was waiting to pick me up.

"Why you have me waitin on you?"

"My mother found out I cut school and she saw my face."

"I unnastand bout school and all dat, cause you a smart girl. I'ma make sho you finish school, but we gotta make moves right now. Know what uhm sayin?"

"Uh huh, but I cain't break curfew no more or miss school or I'ma be in trouble."

"Yeah, well check this out. I'ma drop you off at school. You do good. Don't worry bout nuthin. Then I'ma pick you up tonight so you can know your man's bizness. I'ma pick you up early and I'ma git you home early, so meet me at the spot bout 6:00 tonight."

He picked me up later that evening. There were two carloads of us. One of his partners, Big Moe, was in one car, and me and Andrew in another. We drove around the block of 77th and Euclid a few times, scoping the scene. There were a lot of pretty girls walking up and down the street. One white girl, which I would later learn was Big Moe's girl, the rest Black. Most of them had on fur jackets and mini skirts. One of the Black girls was Fat Bitch. We finally found a spot across the avenue from where the girls walked, that simultaneously hid us but left the action in plain sight. Andrew explained a few things to me:

"You see where the girls walkin?"

"Yeah."

"That's the stroll."

The girls walked sexily near the curbside. They paid total attention to cars driving by. They called out to drivers:

"Hey baby, pull ovah," "Wanna date baby?" as they waved, whistled and wantonly gestured.

Fat Bitch pulled over a car with a white dude inside. He parked around the corner and walked with her inside this massive apartment building. Andrew explained:

"See dat? That's a trick. A trick is a lame muthafucka who have to pay for pussy."

When Fat Bitch and the trick were out of sight, Andrew told me to stay in the car and watch everything, and that I should blow the car horn if I see the Po-leece. Andrew and Big Moe locked eyes and they each jumped out of their cars and went over to the passenger's side of the trick's car. Big Moe had some kinda metal stick that he used to pry open the trick's window. Andrew stuck a wire hanger in the window and after a few tries, they jimmied the window, popped the lock and began searching the car. While Andrew continued to search the car, Big Moe jumped out and headed for another car, one that his White girl had just pulled over. Andrew signaled to me to come over to the car that he was in. When I got there, he handed me a large brown paper bag. He told me to take the bag, stick it down in my pants and hide it in the seat of his car.

A few minutes later, Big Moe and Andrew came back to their cars. They agreed to meet in a few minutes, at Andrew's house, just a few blocks away. When we got there, Andrew pulled out a wad of cash from down in his pants. Big Moe pulled out a gun and a wallet. Andrew's wad was huge. He began counting it out.

"Yeah, nigga see what you almost made us lose. You moves too fast. If I hadn'ta stayed and thoroughly searched that car, we woulda missed out on all lis money."

There was mostly one-hundred dollar bills. Andrew divided the bills into two stacks. They wound up with about a thousand dollars each. Andrew handed Big Moe his half.

Then Big Moe said, "It's only a couple hundred dollars in this wallet, why'on'tchu take all of it and let me keep the gun."

"Dat's cool wit me. Let's go pick up our women case that corner gitting too hot."

Big Moe agreed, but said he had to take his shit home first. He didn't wanna be out with the gun and wad of cash on him.

Andrew said, "Nigga I'on't leave my money in nis house. I takes my shit elsewhere."

Me and Andrew walked out with Big Moe and waited until he pulled off. We got into Andrew's car and he dug down in the seat for the bag that he told me to hide and then we doubled back in the house. When we got inside, Andrew dumped the money out on the bed. There was another $2800 inside. That left Andrew with close to 4 G's. We jumped up and down on the bed for a while.

"See baby, I toldchu, I'ma hustla. We gon' do big thangs. You think I was gon' split all lis wit dat dirty ass nigga? He probably got way more than that gun and that wallet he showed us. Neva trust a nigga in the street, you hear? Don't trust nobody out here, cept me, my brother Lil T, and Fat Bitch. She family. The resta dese niggas and bitches out here is dogs. You hear?"

"Okay."

We headed over to King Kennedy projects over Andrew's mother's house so he could hide the money. When we got back to the stroll, the block was definitely hot. Most of the girls were gone and it was pretty empty.

"Where in the fuck Fat Bitch at? I hope ain't nuthin happen to my bitch." No sooner than he said that, a car horn behind us began blowing us down. Fat Bitch was in the car with some guy. Andrew pulled over and Fat Bitch jumped in the car.

"Get me up outta here. It's hot as hell. That trick I had only wanted to spend $40 and wanted me to lay up in that room wit his ass for more than 10 minutes. I said oh no you gotta give me $60 more dollars if you want all of dat time. He said he had to go outside to get his money out his car. Then he come coming back talking bout he been robbed, somebody broke in his car. I said motherfucka, I sell pussy, I on't got nuthin to do wit dat. If you ain't got no mo money, I gotta go. Then he starts asking me for the $40.00 that he spent back. I told him to kiss my fat black ass. He got all loud and shit and the house manager came and unlocked the door and told him he had to leave. Then the trick gon' go to the corner and call the Po-Leece. The Po-Leece was telling him to stay out from down here. This a bad area, but they was still trying to help this muthafucka. They gon' tell us we betta get off da block cause they was sending the Vice squad after all the hoes. I was so glad when I saw y'all. What took y'all so long?"

Then she looked over at me and said:

"When nis bitch gone start workin? How much y'all get out that trick's car?"

"Who you callin a bitch, yo mama a bitch, bitch!"

"Ladies, ladies, stop this ignunt ass shit. We family. Elaine helped us make money tonite. She a official car tamperer."

"Car tamperer. Her pussy ain't no betta dan mine. Matta fac she'll sell mo cause she new."

"Bitch don't tell me how to run my bidness. I'm bout to take bof uh you ladies home cause I need a good night sleep. Bright and early in the morning, I'ma trade this hunk a junk in, and buy me a new car. How much money you got besides that $40 from that last trick?"

"I got $180 all together."

"Gimme a hundred outta dat. Keep da rest for you and yo kids. You did good for it to still be early. Here go eighty dollars for you too, Big Stuff."

"Oh, no, I can't take that money home. You just hold onto it for me."

Like I said before, my parents were straight up squares and I didn't want Mama to know nothing about me being involved in anything illegal. She woulda died.

"Whatevah you say," Andrew said with a smile in his voice.

We headed toward my neighborhood. I was glad to be going home early, so I wouldn't get in trouble. But I was suspicious that Andrew wasn't really gonna take Fat Bitch home. He had been sneaking around with her a lot. He always lied to me, telling me he was only going to pick money up from her. He always said I was his favorite. But I knew he liked her and I was kinda jealous of their relationship.

I began to enjoy a high degree of success with Andrew's "bidness" ventures. Soon, I knew how to do cars by myself. He had totally cut Big Moe and I was his right hand.

One of the main reasons why Andrew and everybody kinda backed away from Big Moe is because there was a rumor that he shot one of his girls in the head. The girl that got shot in the head was one of my best friends, Pansie, who grew up with me on 68th. I don't know exactly what happened, but I did go see her when I heard about it. That was one of the scariest things in my life.

When I walked in the hospital room, she was lying on her stomach. The doctors had her head in what looked like a space-type contraption. Her head was the size of a giant cantaloupe. It was swollen because they had to cut her head from one ear to the other to get the bullet out. I could see the stitch marks because all of her hair was shaved off. I could also see a big bulge that looked like where the bullet must have gone into her head. I couldn't believe it when she began talking to me.

"What's up Lainey?" she said slowly.

"Pansie. Who did this to you?" I said sorrowfully.

"I on't know."

"Damn, did dis happen to you on the stroll?"

"Something like that. You still wit Andrew?"

"Yeah. He waitin outside. He da one who told me you got shot. I went over yo mother's and she told me I should come and visit you."

"Thanks for comin to see me, Laine."

"Are you hurtin? What did it feel like."

"You know dem big cymbals they play in the orchestra? It

felt and sounded like two of dem just got crashed over my head real hard. And I could hear and feel it. It was ringin in my ears. It was like I was moving in another world. It's the worse."

"Damn."

"I cain't move and I feel tired, Lainey."

"I understand. I'll be back to see you."

"Lainey, be careful out there. You gotta watch yo own back out dere and don't trust nobody. Nobody. I mean it."

"I uh be back to see you soon. I hope you feel betta."

I certainly watched Andrew's back. When he shot dice, I watched his back. When he did breaking and enterings, I watched his back. When he stole cars, I watched his back. By now I was well-seasoned in various aspects of the street life. One night Andrew went out to hit a lick. He said I shouldn't come along this time, that he was gonna do it with his friend, Ricky. He bought me a pizza, a pepsi and a pack of cigarettes and told me to wait at his house until he came back. I waited and waited and waited. Hours and hours went by. I didn't go home. I was too worried about him. I stayed there until I awoke in the morning to Lil T banging on the bedroom door. "Sis, wake up. Andrew on da phone."

I jumped up and ran downstairs to the phone. "Hi baby, when you comin home?"

"I got busted. I need some grands for a lawyer and for my bail. I called Fat Bitch already. I on't wantchu out doing no car tamperings or shooting no dice or nothin while I'm in here. I needchu to work wit Fat Bitch. She'll teach you everything you need to know about the stroll. Hear? She gone keep all the money y'all make every night until y'all got enough to get me outta here. You love me don'tchu?"

"You know I do."

"Well, go wit her every night to work and go straight home. If you make money early, you can go home early, go to school and try to stay in good witcho mama. You my school girl, anyway. I want you to finish. I'ma send you to college. We just doin nis shit til I git on my feet."

That night at dusk, Fat Bitch met me over Andrew's. She pulled up in the front of the house wit some old man, one her regular tricks, I guess.

I had on a skirt, but I wasn't dressed like a hoe. I had on a little make-up, not much.

"You think you gon' make some money dressed like that?" She said when I walked out to get in the car.

I just jumped in the backseat of the car, cause I already knew she didn't like me. The feeling was mutual. We went on Crawford road between Chester and Hough. The dude she had to drive us over there stayed parked out across from the "Hotel" all night. The "Hotel" was actually somebody's rooming house. Fat Bitch explained what she wanted me to know about turning a trick.

"This hotel cost 2 dollas. The object of the game is to get a trick to go in da hotel witchu. Never tell them how much it cost. Start off by letting them tell you how much they can spend. The first law of ho-ing is git yo money first. Hide it under yo wig. Well, you ain't got no wig. Just put it in yo shoe, and don't take yo shoes off. When you get em in the room, try to make em cum fast as you can. Time is money. Make em wash off they dick before you let em stick it anywhere. Always look at it real good and squeeze it. If you see something comin outta dey dick, they got a disease. Never let a muthafucka lay on top of you. A trick shouldn't take no longer than 5 minutes. You know how to use a rubbah?"

"Uh uh."

"I thought you was a dumb bitch. Keep a fresh rubbah in yo mouf at all times. If a muthafucka want you to suck dey dick, work the rubbah over dey dick witout them knowing you got it in yo mouth. Some of dese nasty muthafuckas don't wanna wear no rubbah. If a muthafucka want some pussy, that cost extra and you gotta make em wear a rubbah. You got any?"

"No."

"Here, pay me back after you break luck. The man in the hotel sells em for a dolla a wop. Buy yo own. Get busy."

I kinda knew how to walk. I saw girls walking all the time on the Euclid stroll. Plus, I saw the girls on 95th and Cedar avenue all the time, ever since I was little, since me and Mama used to ride buses pass there when she used to take me to dayswork with her sometimes.

I sashayed up and down the street, looking into cars, waving if I saw a man inside. It wasn't long before somebody pulled over to me. As soon as they did, she come runnin her fat ass over there, "Hey baby, you wanna have a good time, come on wit me."

I had no idea we were in competition. She wanted to make more money than me.

The trick said, "I wanna talk to yo frien. How much you chargin, baby?"

"How much can you spend, I asked? The hotel is $2.

"I got $40 for some pussy."

"Okay. Pull up into the parking lot uh da hotel."

As the young, good-looking Black guy was pulling up into the parking lot and I walked pass Fat Bitch, she chuckled, saying "One thing, I forgot to mention, neva sell no young nigga some pussy. He ain't gonna wanna get up in 5 minutes. And neva get in the car wit a young nigga. Most of em will rob and rape you."

"Thanks," I said.

I found out a lot of stuff I didn't know as the night wore on. You weren't supposed to take off all your clothes. And until you get the knack of it, it was hard to tell when someone ejaculated. Some guys knew how to hide the fact that they'd done it. And they would try to make trouble saying they didn't get their money's worth. Of course, I was new. I was nervous and dumb. One thing I was glad about was that this first guy did not have a huge one and he didn't give me a problem about using a rubber. The bad part was that he didn't want to stop at the end of the 5 minutes and he didn't want to spend no more money. I had to start a loud argument with him and make a scene to get him to let me out the room. One thing about Fat Bitch, she was dedicated to Andrew. She wanted me to have to turn a lot of tricks and make a lot of money, so when she heard me yelling for the trick to let me out of the room, she got the front desk man to open the door and I got out.

I don't remember how much money I made that first night. I just kept handing it over to Fat Bitch after every trick. It was a "good night." Tricks were out in full force and so were the girls and drag queens. I forgot to mention. A lot of drag queens worked the Crawford stroll. I felt a little safer out there knowing that they were there because although they carried themselves like women, they were men. And, some of them were big and strong looking and would shoot or cut a trick that got out of hand. I was always a very friendly person, so the queens liked me. I learned quickly that you had to make friends with people on the street or at least not make enemies. Before the night was over, I had serviced about 10 guys. Not bad for a newbie.

Some dudes tried to touch my breasts or kiss me and they got an attitude at the thought that that was not part of the deal. I always heard Andrew say selling pussy was "bidness" not pleasure and I was strickly about the business of trying to help Andrew get out of jail. I was Big Stuff, his partner in crime.

We hit the stroll every night for about a week. I was living a double life. School each day, stroll each night. I was kinda grateful that Drew's primary identity was not a pimp and that I only turned tricks occasionally. I almost got arrested for prostitution once while I was with Drew, but by the grace of God the detective let me go. I lied to him, saying I wasn't working. I told him that I made money by going to the store for the working ladies and that I was going home to get my school clothes ready. He let me go with a strict warning that if he ever saw me out late at night, he was gonna have me put away in the bad girls' home.

Lil T had hooked up with a woman that also worked the stroll and he agreed to watch out for us, take us out there and bring us home every night until Drew got out. One night a trick tried to rob Lil T's woman. The trick had walked up out of nowhere and asked Lil T's woman for a date. They agreed on a price and when she turned to walk with him to the hotel, he pushed her back up against this house and told her to give him all of her money or he would cut her. She gave him her wig and her purse. He took off running down the street. Lil T was parked right across the street in a parking lot. He saw the guy running and raised up outta his car with a sawed off shotgun, shot up in the air and yelled "Stop or I'll blow yo ass away." The robber stopped in his tracks. When Lil T walked up on him the robber threw the wig towards Lil T and started apologizing, saying he ain't have no money or no food and begging for forgiveness. But in the streets, you can't appear to have a heart. Lil T blasted off two shots, one in each of the robber's legs. I never heard a man cry like that. Loretta (Lil T's woman) and I screamed and cried too. We had no idea T was gonna shoot the dude. In a flash T was gone.

After that night, I really wasn't ever wantin to go back out there. I asked Fat Bitch how close we were to getting Drew out because seeing Loretta get robbed and that man get shot did something to me.

The very next day, as I walked home from school, I heard a car slowing down beside me and a familiar voice:

"Big Stuff, get over here."

It was Andrew! I was so happy to see him. I ran over to the car and hopped in.

"Baby, you my bad bitch. My lawyer got me out today. He a fixer. Time he get through paying folks off, I'll beat this little punk-ass case. But I need you and Fat Bitch to keep workin the stroll a few more weeks. You still love yo man, don't you?"

"You know I do, but I ain't goin back on no stroll."

"Yeah, I heard about what happened. I got something else for you. I want you to work with Candy. She my homeboy's girl. She a class A sneak-thief. She don't do no whole lotta flatbacking. Fat Bitch ain't wanna learn how to be a good thieving hoe, she rather flatback for hers. But you, I know you got larceny in yo heart. Once you learn how to get a trick's money out his wallet witout him even knowing it, you gon' be one of the baddess bitches in this town."

I thought, *Okay, after he gets out of this trouble, I won't have to do none of this no more.* Andrew picked me up a little earlier than usual. When I got in the car, a guy was sitting in the front and Fat Bitch was in the back.

"Big Stuff, you need some sexier clothes and a wig. We goin to another stroll downtown. The tricks that be down through there got mo' money and you gotta look the part. How you like this? Give it to her baby." He motioned to Fat Bitch to give me the outfit and the wig they'd bought for me.

"You need to take that ponytail down and throw a couple braids in your hair before you put this wig on. Always wear a stocking cap under yo wig. It's good for holding yo money," said Fat Bitch.

"I like the dress and the wig but I can't take this home at the end of the night."

"Don't worry, just change back into your school clothes and leave that in the car," said Andrew.

"Okay."

Before long, we were at someone's house. Andrew's homie, Fox, went in and came back in a few minutes.

"Hey man, you want yo little broad to change clothes ovah here? My woman can hook up her make-up and shit."

"Thanks, mane."

"Big Stuff, go in there and get ready."

The house we went in was nice. All the furniture was slick. Not corny Victorian-looking furniture, but swanky, hip stuff that rich cool people would have. The paintings on the walls were different than any I'd ever seen. Silhouettes of naked Black men and women's bodies. African art; plants, swanky lamps and chandeliers. TV's all over the place, plush carpet. Fresh everything. Into the living room area walks this young, beautiful, light brown-skinned lady. She had a figure that wouldn't wait. She wore a tight fitting short black evening-type dress, high heels. She had a cute little black handbag that matched her heels. She dressed better than any of the girls or drag queens I'd seen on Euclid, Crawford, or Cedar. She was a goddess, a movie star.

"Candy, dis my homeboy Andrew's woman. What's yo name, baby?"

"Big Stuff," I said.

"She gone work witchu tonite. Cool?"

"It's cool. She know how to work?"

"Naw, she new, but Andrew say she got a heart like a lion."

"That's what they all say, til the deal go down," she said as she looked me up and down.

"I hope you ain't wearin *that* to work with me."

"Naw, my dress and my wig in this bag."

"Let me see. That's cute. Let me hook you up. Come upstairs," she said as she grabbed my hand and led me upstairs to her bathroom.

"Always be freshly showered before you go to work and wear the best cologne, lotion and lingerie you can afford. If you want men to spend money, you have to look, smell and taste the part. Keep your nails and your toes done, too. All of that adds value to you. Know what Ahm saying?"

"Yeah."

"If you look like a regla Black girl, you gone git regla Black money. I gets white girl money. That I don't make, I take, you dig?"

"Yeah," I said matter-of-factly.

"Here's some shower stuff. When you come out, we'll take it from there."

I took a nice hot shower which I thoroughly enjoyed. All the places I ever lived only had baths. A shower was a rarity. Plus, her toiletries were nice. When I came out, she had my dress and wig laid out, and several pairs of shoes for me to choose from.

"I hope yo feet ain't too big. I wear a size 7. After I hook up your nails, make-up and wig, see if you can wear a pair of my shoes. Them thangs you got on gone block dollas."

After lavishing in her lotions and colognes, she proceeded to do my nails for me.

"Damn, how many different colognes you put on? You ain't spose to mix em dummy. You only spose to use one kind. You smell like a fuckin perfume shop."

"Sorry, dayum. I ain't know," I said with half-way hurt feelings.

"It's cool. I did the same damn thang when I ain't know no betta," she said as she giggled. I liked her cause she didn't call me a bitch and she seemed free hearted, like me.

"How old is you?"

"Old enough."

"You sho is, dummy. You old enough to get killed. You probably ain't no older than 16. If you don't wanna tell me, it's cool. I'm only 17 myself. It ain't yo age that matters, it's how much sense you got out here. Somebody had to teach me. See, it's a lotta young broads out here, ain't got nobody to teach em nuthin and they just out here, giving the game a black eye. You gotta have class witcho shit. And never give a nigga all of yo money. Cause, I don't care how much shit a nigga talk about he love you and you his bottom woman, that muthafucka will leave yo ass witout shit. I been down for mine since I was twelve. I got a baby wit Fox. My mama keeps her for us. Everything in this place is in my mama's name. It's all mine. If Fox go to jail or get killed or anything happen, this my shit. My mama keeps a bank account for me and my baby. Ain't no nutha broad comin up in here. I don't play dat wife-in-law shit. If Fox got a nutha bitch out dere, he betta keep it outta my face. You got wife-in-laws?"

"I guess."

"You ain't spose to be guessing out here. You gotta know where you stand wit a nigga."

While Candy was schooling me to her version of the game, she was steadily giving me a make over. When I looked in the mirror, I was drop-dead gorgeous! I didn't even know I could look like that. I knew Candy and I would get along well. I liked her style. Candy said we would be going downtown to the Sheraton hotel. Some type of business convention was in town and there'd be a bunch of men with money looking for girls.

"Now, this is how it's goin down. I do all the talkin. I'ma get a trick to take bof of us into a room. Whatever I tell you to do, you gotta do it. You gotta be able to read my eyes, if I can't tell you something. Try to keep the trick distracted. Put yo pussy or yo titties in his mouf. Never let him be studying what Ahm doin cause I'ma be gittin his money out of his wallet. We let him get naked, but we don't get naked. When I give you the hi sign it's time to go, move out. You got dat Miss Lion Heart?"

"I got it."

When we came back downstairs, Fat Bitch, Andrew and Fox were sitting in the living room listening to *Hustler's Convention*, laughin and talkin. When I came in the room, I could see the hatred of my guts in Fat Bitch's eyes. I was lookin good. Not like a tennis shoe hoe, but a real life pro. Andrew's eyes were all over me, but he couldn't brag on me too much. Fat Bitch was sitting there ready to go off.

"Candy say the money gone be at the Sheraton tonite. We can't be lurking and lingering around down there, Andrew. You can't do no car tampering round there and all the girls have to work inside. Ain't no strollin round there. White folks don't play dat shit down there. Run off the good tricks. This spot is sweet, " Fox says, kissing his fingers Mama Mia Italian style.

"Cool wit me," said Andrew.

"Y'all can drop me off on 21st and Prospect. That's where Ahm working tonight," said Fat Bitch.

"Let's roll!" Andrew said.

Candy and I got dropped off downtown at the Sheraton. It was a real swanky joint. Lots of men and women sitting around the bar and at tables. We sashayed up to the bar and before we could get the bartender's attention, these two White guys in business suits were trying to get our attention—winking, smiling, and waving. One of them came over to me and asked me to dance with him. I looked at Candy for the okay. She nodded in agreement and when I walked by her she whispered, "Don't talk too much." I headed out to the dance floor and began to dance as smoothly as possible with my partner.

"What's your name," he asked.

"You can call me Big Stuff."

"I'm Jack. What are you and your girlfriend doing tonite?"

"Partying."

"That's good, because my friend and I are looking for some beautiful women to party with. Do you wanna come up to our room? We can have some drinks and whatever we feel like doing."

"I don't know, I'll have to see what my girlfriend feels like doing."

"It looks like she's in the partying mood. Look, she's on the floor with my buddy."

At the end of the song, Candy and I went back to our drinks at the bar.

"Finish up. Dese boys is spendin. I told the one I was dancing wid, we need $500 each and they can have the rest of our time for tonite. We don't split up. We all gone party in the same room. If they got a grand, they got way more. We fuck em til they tired. We don't drink no more. We pour water in our drinks or keep dumpin out our glasses. Let dem get drunk. When they pass out, we get da rest of what's in they wallets and move out. Let's sell pussy."

We walked over toward our dates and headed upstairs to a room and what Candy said is how it went down. We played wit em, danced for em, switched up, let em drink up, sexed em up, ripped em off and got out. My first night in the "big leagues."

•5•
Breakin Free
(for a minute)

I WAS PUTTING MAMA through hell. By now, if I was out past curfew, sometimes I just stayed out. My grades were horrible. I used to be a good student. I participated in extracurricular activities—choir, orchestra, junior varsity cheerleading. Now, I didn't care that much about school anymore. Sometimes I would go to school after being out all night hustling with Andrew or Candy. It got to the point where I would try to sneak in the house when no one was home so that I could get school clothes.

Mama used to be my best friend. She bought me everything. Things she never had for herself growing up poor in Jamaica. Mama had a lot of ambition, but no "oppachunity." Mama wanted whatever part of the American dream she could have, too—a family, a decent life, a home for us, an education, success. Daddy usta say that Mama just wanted to be like her other Jamaican friends. Daddy said he didn't want the headache of owning "one a dese rat trap houses. Let that Jew worry bout the upkeep uh one a dese dayum traps." But that didn't stop her dream. Mama kept right on working and saving. Ole skool Jamaicans can save 3 cents out of a nickel! Remember I told you how Mama was able to pay for my abortion in New York. Mama and Daddy wanted us to be something, but their methods of encouragement were different. Anytime we did anything wrong, Daddy would say, "Y'all niggas is the best I seen yet. Y'all ain't gone mount ta nuthin noway." Mama hated when he said that to us:

"Gilly, don't tell di children dat. Don't put yo mout on dem. Nigga mout is like goat. Anyting it touch, it spoil. Yuh will mark dem."

Mama did everything she could to give us "oppachunity." The white folks that Mama worked for gave us expensive gently worn hand-me-downs. She picked out nice pieces from those and sent some to Jamaica, too. And on top of that, Mama bought us nice clothes to wear to church and school. Although Mama didn't speak "PropaHinglish" she knew what it sounded like and she always had something to say about how we should talk. She tried her best to keep tabs on us. She took me to Jamaica every summer, so that I was never left unattended in the states. She tried to shield and protect me the best she could. After all of her protecting and supportiveness, I still got pregnant. And even then, when I begged her to not let me have the baby, she went through hell and high water to help me seek a safe and professional abortion.

But now, it was like me and Mama hated each other. She couldn't stand the sight of me and I couldn't stand to hear her mouth. She was the worst person in the world. Why? Because she wanted me to go to school. Because she tried to find out where I was and what I was doing and she always wanted me to be home at a decent time of night. But Elaine was troubled. I didn't know who or what I was becoming or why I was doing the things that I did or why my life was going the way it was. I was becoming Mama's worst nightmare.

Through Mama's meddling and God's grace, I managed to not totally drop out of school. By now, I was coming toward the end of 8th grade. I was bright enough to come to classes periodically, not do the homework and still pass my classes with C's. I did fail one of my classes—algebra. By now, Mama was at her wits end.

One day when I came home from cuttin school, Mama was waiting for me. (As I said before, Mama was a cleaning lady at my junior high school and she worked second shift and was never home when I got there. I was a latchkey girl.)

"Mi ago kill yuh. Yuh nuh want nuttin from life? Before I mek a dutty nigga ruin yuh life, mi will kill yuh mi-self and walk downtown and tell the dyam police is mi kill yuh."

As she finished her words, Mama swung viciously from behind her back with a black leather strap and tried to lash me, but I grabbed the belt and wouldn't let go.

"O, a wha dis fadda God? Let go uh a di belt gyal."

"Naw, Mama I ain't takin no whuppin. I'm too old for dat. Don't hit me!" I cried.

"Let go uh a di belt, mi sey," she said deliberately enunciating every syllable.

But I just stood there holding the belt, and crying. The next thing I know, I saw lightening again. Mama dropped the belt and socked me dead in the eye with her raw fist. She hit me so hard, I fell to the floor.

"Go wash up! If you can't live here by dese rules, you can live by the White pipo rules." Little did I know that Mama had made a deal with the Juvenile authorities. She had a family friend waiting outside. When I finished doctoring on my fresh black eye, Mama led me outside and pushed me into her friend's car. I didn't know where we were going; but I soon learned, it was the Juvenile Home on 22nd near Cedar.

When we got there, they asked Mama a bunch of questions and filled out paperwork. I just sat there, trying to be hard but halfway wanting to bust out crying. The next thing I know, I was led away from Mama into a big room with a bunch of kids. Some of the kids were crying, others were playing and laughing.

An old four-eyed, pot belly, corny looking White man in a gray suit came over to me and began talking:

"Hello, Elaine. My name is Frank Johnson. I have been assigned your case. It seems you'll be living here for a while. Why don't you like your own home?"

"None uh yo business."

"It's okay, Elaine. You don't have to tell me anything. You can stay here as long as it takes. You see a lot of the kids here… they don't have a mom who is trying to save their life. Your mom and dad have to work to take care of you and all they want you to do is go to school and stay out of trouble. But your mom tells me you are having a hard time doing that. What happened to your eye?"

"None uh yo business."

"Well, I am here every day until 5:30 p.m. If you ever wanna talk, I'll be around. Someone will get around to you shortly to show you where everything is and to give you pajamas and supplies."

Bastard! I don't need no supplies and pajamas, I thought to myself. *Damn, I need to talk to Andrew and tell him to get me outta here. They got me locked up in juvie.* I sat there for a while looking at the other kids and brooding. Pretty soon my hard armour began to crack. I couldn't use the phone. And I couldn't get comfortable. I didn't want to talk to anyone. I just wanted to get out. Who could help me? God. Maybe if I asked God to forgive me, he would help me get out. I started cryin, prayin and askin God to get me out.

"Lord, please get me outta here. I don't wanna be locked up

with dese kids. God, I know I been bad but I am not a bad person. If you let me get outta here, I'ma do better. I promise."

I cried and cried and cried and cried and cried and cried. Finally, Mr. Johnson came back.

"Are you ready to talk, Elaine?"

"Yes," I sobbed, "I wanna go home."

"Why are you here? Your mom tells me you were a good student, but you don't like school anymore."

"I do like school. It's just that sometimes I hafta miss because I have to be with my boyfriend to help him."

"Why do you have to help him?"

"Because I love him. We're best friends. He needs me."

"What does he need you to do with him? Did he hit you?"

"No, I got hit by my mother. I just stay with him and be his friend, cause his life is hard and he needs somebody to love him and we care about each other."

"How old is your boyfriend, Elaine?"

Andrew was 18 then, but I couldn't tell them the truth because they would say he was too old for me. So, I lied:

"We the same age."

"Does he go to school?"

"Yes."

"Elaine, I don't know why his parents don't have him here if the both of you are cutting school and breaking curfew. If you don't straighten up, you'll be getting sent away and then you won't get to see your boyfriend for a long time. Would you like that?"

"No, I wanna go home. Tell my Mama to please let me come back home. I won't cut school or break curfew again, I promise," I sobbed.

"Okay, Elaine. Your mom and I made a deal. She brought you down here so you could see what would happen to you if you don't straighten up. You can't worry about helping Andrew. You have to help yourself. If his parents are okay with him staying out all night and not going to school, then he will suffer in the long run; but your mom wants you to go to school and make something of your life. I told your mom that I'd bring you home if you make a deal with me. Elaine, you have to promise me that you won't miss another day of school, you won't cut class, you won't break curfew and you will come home every night. Can you promise me that, Elaine?"

"Yes, yes. I won't be bad no more. I'ma do good in school and I won't stay out late or stay out all night. I promise."

"Shake on it."

I shook hands with Mr. Johnson and he took me home. I was so glad to be home. I wouldn't be able to help Andrew anymore. I had to do everything right. Not only did I promise Mr. Johnson and Mama, I promised God. Andrew would have to understand.

The phone kept ringing—2 rings, hang-up, 1 ring. Andrew was looking for me, but I couldn't answer and Mama didn't either. When she got tired of it ringing, she just took it off the hook.

"Yuh haffi stop seeing dat no good nigga Andrew, yuh 'ear? I know who he is and if yuh nuh stop see im, you know what ago hap'm?"

"Yes, Mama."

For the next few days, Mama walked me to school. Andrew would drive by us, but he couldn't stop and I could only glance out of the corner of my eye as me and Mama made it up to Central Jr. High. Andrew resorted to sending me messages through Josephine.

"Andrew told me to tell you that you gotta make a way to see him."

"Tell him, I'll see him as soon as I can, but if I mess up, I'ma get sent up. I ain't tryna get sent away. I'll figure out sumpthin soon."

Around this time, Mama also got me a Big Sister. You know the program that provides youth with a mentor, someone to talk to about stuff you don't feel you can discuss with your parents. My mentor was a very attractive coffee-cream colored young Black woman. Her name was Lynn Wilson. Lynn was a college student. She wore her hair permed, parted to one side, curled and cut into a nice neat style. She wore very little make-up and lipstick. She had straight white teeth and a big smile. Although she was nice to me, I didn't feel I could open up to her and tell her everything I was thinking, doing and going through. Lynn tried hard to help me. She would ask me about my relationship with Andrew, and she tried not to make me feel like I was under investigation.

"So, this Andrew must be quite the good-looking guy? What about him makes you like him so much?"

"I don't know. He is very cute. We spend a lot of time together. He tells me all of his dreams and plans about his life and what we are going to have and do when we get ourselves together. We're just best friends."

"What kinds of things do you do together?"

"Everything."

"Like what?"

"We hang out. We take long rides. We listen to music together, go to the drive-in. Stuff like that."

"Does he ever ask you to do things that you don't want to do?"

"No."

"So, all the times you stayed out late, broke curfew, stayed away from home, or skipped school—you wanted to do those things yourself and he never said you shouldn't do it?"

"Right. I do everything with him because I want to be with him."

"If someone cares about you, they don't want you to do anything that is not good for you. He isn't good for you, Elaine, if he doesn't encourage you to go to school and stay home with your parents. You are not an adult. How old is he?"

"We the same age."

"Look, we are young women. We have to take care of ourselves. You are a pretty and intelligent girl, Elaine. You have a lot to offer. You have to take care of yourself. Do what is good for you. Your family loves you. That's why your mom asked me to be your big sister. You should be involved in positive activities. Wanna go to Euclid Beach with me?"

"Yeah. That might be fun."

"Might be? Since you so big and bad and love to stay out late, I know you ain't scared to ride on every roller coaster out there are you?"

"Me, scared? You don't know who you talkin to. They call me Big Stuff."

Lynn took me to Euclid Beach. We had a ball. She called me all the time. She helped me with homework. Lynn was picking me up and taking me to school. She was always talking to me about loving myself and how beautiful I was. I began to talk to her a little bit. I told her Andrew was the first guy that liked me. I told her we had sex and that we loved each other. She asked me if we used protection and if I was on birth control. I told her yes.

Somehow I couldn't tell her that I was turning tricks, stealing, and feeling like I couldn't get out of it. There was a part of me that enjoyed this life, all the while I knew I should do better. But, I didn't feel good about myself. For one thing, I had acne, my hair was short and I didn't feel pretty on the inside. I was just a "regla" Black girl. My parents loved me and I had a stable family. I wasn't molested or neglected by my family, I just didn't love myself.

I was going to school regularly now and Andrew stopped calling so much and he stopped driving by the house.

I heard from Josephine that Andrew had caught another case. This time he was in jail for receiving stolen property. Josephine said Andrew wanted me to get in touch with Fat Bitch. I told her I would, but I didn't. Andrew sent me his address through Josephine and I began to write him while he was in county jail. He would be fussing, asking me to hook up with Fat Bitch so that we could get some money together to help him beat his case. I kept telling him I would do it, but I wouldn't. I would write him poems, copy down lyrics from love songs and send him pictures, but I wouldn't do any street hustling.

I was enjoying hanging out with Lynn and going to school. I started walking to school with Josephine sometimes or by myself again. Andrew had been locked up for a few months. Everything was going fine. I was now in the ninth grade. Mama had bought me some new school clothes. My most prized possession among them though was my new tan leather midi-coat with matching boots. I was the most stylish "regla" Black chick in Cleveland, Ohio, when I wore that git up.

One day, as I walked to the end of 68th and onto Clarkwood near Central Ave, I heard Andrew's voice. He jumped out of the car and walked over to me:

"What's up, Big Stuff? Miss me baby?"

He looked so good. His skin and eyes had cleared up in jail since he hadn't been drinking Boone's Farm, smoking weed and poppin pills we called seecos. Although he had just got out of jail and it was early in the morning, I could tell that he had got his daily dosage into his system. When he was high, it didn't take much for him to go into a rage. I wanted to hug him and tell him how much I still loved him, but I was scared:

"How come you ain't git in touch wit Fat Bitch?"

"I had to go to school. I cain't get in no more trouble or I'ma git sent up. I told you."

"So, you was just gone let a nigga rot in jail, huh? You been fuckin somebody else?"

"Why you say that. You know betta dan that."

"I on't know shit. All I know is ain't nobody seen you. Come on. Get in the car."

"I can't go witchu. I have to go to school."

"Since when you start tellin me what you gone do. I said get in the car."

"I cain't do it, Drew."

I was actually happy that Andrew had been in jail. I enjoyed the down time. He was pissed because I didn't respond to his commands about working to get him out of jail. Plus, I had avoided him, by not answering my phone, and I had dodged him by walking different routes to and from school with Mama and getting rides from Lynn until he got locked up.

"Bitch, you thank uhm stupid." He grabbed me and pulled the lapels of my tan leather coat apart, until all the buttons popped off.

"Stop it muthafucka. You tearin up my new coat my mother bought!"

"You thank uhm stupid, bitch. I know you fuckin somebody else," he said as he began swinging on me. I started running but I couldn't out run him. He caught me and flung me down to the ground. He stomped and kicked me. I just balled up in the fetal position, screaming and crying outta control. He stood over me:

"Bitch, teach yo ass a lesson. Dat's yo muthafuckin school right dere!"

Then he jumped in his car and sped off.

I was glad he left me. I limped back toward my house like a tattered soldier. I couldn't go to school. I was sore and bruised and what hurt more than anything was that he jacked up my leather coat. Mama bought me that coat to show me that she was proud of me going to school and staying out of trouble. I hated Andrew for tearing up my new coat.

When I went back home, Mama was there. By now, she had quit doing dayswork jobs and only worked at Central Jr. High. When I walked in the door. Mama screamed:

"Uhhh, dat dutty nigga!"

She jumped right on the phone and called the police. They came over to take my statement. I said I didn't know who jumped me. I said two guys that I never saw before jumped out of a car and jumped me. I made up some phony info about the color of the car, the year and make. Mama knew I was lying. But I didn't want to tell on Andrew. I knew he was gonna get his.

Later that afternoon a brick came crashing through our living room window. Good thing no one was sitting in there. That was Andrew's way of letting me know, that he wasn't finished with me. After that day, Lynn started riding me to and from school again.

A few weeks later, Josephine told me that Andrew got sentenced to 4 to 25 years in prison. I was glad. It gave me a chance to get free. He controlled me, and I let him. I felt obligated to stay with him. In my mind, I couldn't leave him. He was my first love.

But when I was away from him I felt relieved. I could do simple stuff like go to school regularly. I could go places with Lynn, and Mama and I got along.

Andrew began writing me from prison. He told me how much he loved me and was going to marry me when he got out. He apologized for everything that he ever did to me. He promised he would never hit me again. He promised that he was not gonna be living the streetlife no more and that he wanted me to finish school. He wrote some of the best Jail Talk on the planet.

Elaine Ball, my wife. A beautiful young woman that every man on this earth would be proud to have. I will never lie to you or do you wrong because you would never do that to me. I'm gonna get a job and take care of you. I'm gonna send you to school and let you get an education because I need you to be smart to run our business. Send me pictures. I miss your pretty face, your soft lips, your big legs and your BIG STUFF. SMILE.

He drew me beautiful pictures. He had the best handwriting of any boy I had ever seen.

In the beginning, I wrote and visited him faithfully for the first year while he was in Mansfield Reformatory. I would go along with Mrs. Ball and use his sister's birth certificate; but eventually, I stopped writing and visiting.

I started liking my new life of going to school regularly. I went to summer school and repeated the Algebra class that I had failed, and I got an A. That felt good. Mama reminded me that I could get A's anytime if I put my mind to it. I got active in choir and started back playing my violin, even though I had to play on one that I borrowed from the school. I donated my violin to Andrew (which he sold to buy some get high). I had also donated Daddy's gun to Andrew. Ditto.

If Mama had given up on me, I probably wouldn't have graduated from Central Junior High, and moved on to East Tech. I was single throughout high school. I tried to focus on being a regular student hoping that nobody would make the link between me and Big Stuff. Choir was my favorite subject. Our choir teacher noticed my voice and began giving me solo parts to sing. When she wanted certain parts to be strong or just the way she wanted, she'd hook me up with certain other kids who sang well. Two of the other girls became my good friends, Tanya and Netie. Tanya told us about her sister, Darlene, who also sang but went to a different school and I had another friend, Danette, who had the voice of a lark. I don't even remember how I met Danette. But that girl could sang! Together we became the Five Shades of Love. We loved singing. We rehearsed every single day. Tanya and Darlene lived kinda close to me, so Tanya and I would stop by my house after school, eat. Then we'd walk to her house, eat again and we'd all get together and rehearse. When we got tight enough, we auditioned for Cleveland's biggest talent show: Miss Ross's East Tech Talent Show. Kids from all over the city, not just Tech, participated in Miss Ross's shows. It was a big deal. Groups and singers like Earl Gaye and the Imaginations, The Executioners, Cash, Brown Sugars, The Deltones, Conway Owens, Diane Woods, The Devastating Dreams, Four of a Kind... The list just went on and on. These shows gave young talent in Cleveland a positive outlet and training. Miss Ross didn't take no stuff. She believed in excellence. Clevelanders ranked her talent show equal or better than the Apollo, because at Miss Ross' shows no one booed. That's because if you weren't good, she wouldn't put you on. To this day, I am still grateful for the lessons that she taught us.

"Nevah let the audience get tired of you. I don't give a damn if you Michael Jackson, after 20 minutes, Ahm tired uh yo ass!"

And she only gave 20 minute slots to the groups that she felt were good enough to be "Special Guest." She only gave that honor to one or two groups per show. Now mind you, Miss Ross's show was not a competition and there were no prizes or money to be made. Your reward was the roar of the crowd and people giving you love every time you came out of the house. You became a ghetto superstar if you rocked WHK Auditorium! That was reward enough for us. Our group was a big hit. After a few years, she finally chose the Five Shades of Love to be guest stars. This was no small accomplishment.

Our group began singing all over town. You might say we were EnVogue before EnVogue or Destiny's Child before Destiny's Child. The only difference was our parents didn't know how to direct us to people who could get us to a national level. Word on the street was, the only way out of Cleveland was through the O'Jays and we didn't have a link to them. The Brown Sugars did, but they never blew up. The only group from that era to get out of Dodge was Kinsman Dazz aka The Dazz Band. But us, we were superstars stuck in the ghetto. It was like being all dressed up with nowhere to go. These were the days before everybody and they mama had a studio in their bedroom or basement.

I had a great experience at East Tech. I was a cheerleader. I went to all the football and basketball games. And the fights, O! To this day, I still remember all the names the John F. Kennedy High School kids called us—"welfare queens," "food stamp babies," "project niggas." Sometimes the fights got out of hand, sometimes people got robbed or stabbed, but mostly, it was plain old rivalry. I was in a vocational education track, an Accounting and Computing major. Although I had potential, I was never one of the students chosen for Upward Bound or any college enrichment. Certain kids got pushed, others didn't.

My parents didn't know how to advocate for me. They had to trust the school. After graduating from East Tech, I figured, I might as well go to college. My reason? Everybody says "education is the key," so I figured I better go. My parents were very happy for this decision. I didn't have any direction. All I knew was I wanted to make something out of my life, but that was about it.

I really wanted to be a singer. But I sure didn't want to end up singing in Gong Shows and smoky bars for the rest of my life. Not even knowing what to major in, I figured, "If Ahm gone go to college, I might as well go to Cleveland State." In my mind, the local community college, wasn't for me. I wanted to go to a real college! And Cleveland State University was it. Although I had a pretty decent high school record, I didn't do well on the ACT and SAT, so I was admitted to CSU's Remedial Program, Special Studies, otherwise known as Student Support Services and TRiO. The program was designed to help poor and first generation college students gain access to higher education and skills.

How could I be placed into dummy classes? I passed Algebra, reading, writing, but for some reason, I didn't do well enough on the college entrance tests to go into regular university classes, so I had to take remedial everything. That put a bad taste in my mouth from the git go.

College was a whole nother world from high school. First of all, everybody has an assigned counselor to help you choose classes. Since I was in Special Studies, my counselor suggested that I take all the remedial courses and general university required courses first. I gave my counselor, Frank, the blues. He would say I had to take this or the other class and I'd tell him that I didn't want to. For one thing, I didn't like nobody telling me what to do. I was grown.

"Okay, I'll sign up for these lil dumb ass classes. I'll be glad when I git out of Special Studies."

And Frank said:

"I'll be glad when you get out of here, too. In fact, I am praying that you make it out of here."

After you get your classes, you have to buy all these expensive ass books and some of them are heavy as hell, and I could hardly get any sense out of them. Because of this, I hardly ever cracked em open, although I did like carrying them around sometimes. They gave me that smart college-chick look.

College is so big that you might not have any classes with people that you went to high school with. I didn't have a high school clique to hang out with. I didn't know where I fit in on campus. I was from da hood. What do I do in between classes? I went to the Black Cultural Center and I didn't fit in with the people who hung out in there. It seemed to me that only the boojie Black students from Cleveland-corny-ass-Heights hung out in there. I wandered kinda aimlessly around campus.

The action in my neighborhood was much more real than cracking open a whitewashed lifeless-ass grammar book. I'll never forget about Koo Koo. She was a sweet nice quiet neighborhood girl, barely in her teens. Never really went anywhere. Just to school and home. She grew up in a house with a lot of relatives, a lot of alcohol. Out of the blue, Koo Koo was pregnant. Nobody seemed to know how she got that way. Next thing you know, Koo Koo was going with her oldest sister's husband. They just kinda came out in the open with it afterwhile. Her oldest sister went off the deep end. Started getting high a lot and runnin the streets. Koo Koo has more kids for this guy. Her kids and her sisters kids are both brothers and sisters and cousins. Koo Koo's mind was totally under her brother-in-law-boyfriend's control.

Koo Koo was saved temporarily when her brother-in-law-boyfriend went to jail. While he's in there, Koo Koo grows up, cleans up her life and finds another boyfriend outside the family. But this two timing, no good, pedophile boyfriend never gave up on the idea that she was his. Word was that he'd write all the time and tell her:

"Bitch, if I cain't have you, nobody will."

He got out and killed her.

The dots wasn't connecting between Cleveland State and everyday life. I found a place on campus that filled the gap and it was called the Shire. It quickly became my favorite spot on campus. There I could hang with people, who drank, smoked weed and kicked it about life. Pretty soon I was in with the partying crowd, and I was partying much more than I was studying—on and off campus.

Off campus, I began to get hip to more after hour joints. Not the little neighborhood watering holes like the ones on 68th. There were others, where the cool people hung out—all the playas, hoes, pimps, number men, hit men, drug dealers, stuff players, entertainers, shot callers, and wannabees. I loved being around these people. That is where I met AC—in an after hour joint. He was tall and fine and that was enough criteria for me.

•6•
Under the Big Top, I Mean the Big Time

I NEVER HAD ENOUGH of nothing. I loved being on the set. I'd take a couple puffs off a spliff and suck on a cute named wine cooler, but being in the ozone was a ways off.

I reconnected with the twins Jean and Jayne, who used to live in the neighborhood back in the day. I loved hanging out with them. They were older than me. *Baad* cain't describe the half of the twins. They were gorgeous—petite, café-au lait complexioned, cute in the face and slim in the waist. And they could hook up some wigs, weaves, and hairstyles that'd make yo head spin. Sassy as all get out. They were small but they could box. They had a rep for snatchin barmaids over the bar and slappin the sound out of bigger women's mouths. Everywhere they went, drama was sure to go. Now Vincent's was *the* place to be. It was the most well-respected after hour joint in Ohio. You might see anybody up in there. Leon Spinks, Don King, Jayne Kennedy.

You didn't just go up in there any kinda way. You had to be sharp. Cain't nobody outdress Black folks. I'm just sorry. A brother or sister's lights might be off, but you wouldn't know it. The fly millionaire look was the goal. The twins hooked me up.

They made up my face, did my hair, nails, toes and made sure that my outfit was right.

It was a Friday night and Vincent's was packed to capacity. But the doorman was immediately persuaded by the twins' beauty to let us in. All eyes were on us as we entered. It was thick, but brothers thinned out a path for us that led to a table near the bar. As soon as we sat down a hostess came over:

"That gentleman over dere say anythang y'all drinking is on him."

"I'll have a Pink Champale."

"Baby girl, dis Vincent's. Drank that cheap shit when you at home. She' uh take your best white wine and so will I," Jayne interrupted.

"I'll have a 151 and coke," ordered Jean.

A few minutes after we got our drinks, "the gentleman" who paid for them came over and introduced himself:

"Good evening lovely ladies. They call me Diamond Dan. I thought I had the best of everything in this life, until now," Diamond said, as he beckoned for my hand to kiss. I held out my hand, smiling and styling my eyes as wide and sexy and cute as I could:

"I'm Elaine," I said, as he kissed my hand and redirected his eyes to the twins.

"I'm Jayne," she said as he kissed her hand, while she purred.

"And you are the finest thang God ever made," he said, saving his prey for last, as he knelt down in front of Jean and waited for her hand.

"Uh huh, huh, I'm Jean."

"Baby, you the woman that's gone change my life. Do you mind if I join you?"

"I don't mind. Y'all mind?"

Jayne and I both shook our heads in approval. Jayne moved over to make space for him to sit near Jean. Since Jean was now giving her full attention to Diamond, Jayne and I began people watching, checkin out the fashion show.

"Girl, you see that baad ass bag that broad got and her shoes? That's what Ahm talking bout. That bag by itself prolly cost around 400 bucks. That's why you have to be bout ya bizness out here. Know what I'm sayin? Cause either you gone be a major playa or a poot butt. Now she prolly sell dope wit her man. Me, I ain't goin out like dat cause I cain't do no time. I ain't met a muthafucka yet, that ain't got busted. You look around, in a year or two, you won't see her ass no mo, bitch uh be done went to Marysville. I got kids. I cain't go to nobody's penitentiary. It's a lot ways out here to get big money witout th'owin bricks at the penitentiary."

Jayne and Jean dreamt big. Jayne always had some type of get rich quick scheme going. She'd always be asking people to borrow their social security number or get a phone in they name. She was a cosmetologist, a barmaid, an interior decorator, a contractor. Jayne of all trades. The biggest was playing niggas, or at least, she thought she was playin em. Her motto was: "If a nigga cain't help you, what you need him fa?" This philosophy sometimes led her to deal with men that she didn't necessarily like, but she needed for something. Once she got all she could, on to the next. Jean was also multi-talented. She did some modeling here and there, retail clothing, very artsy and creative. She was the type that could take a Goodwill outfit that cost $2 and make it designer status. One thing about Jayne and Jean, they were way too slick for pimps and playas. They would snort the caine, drink the wine, enjoy the song, dance and romance, but they never fell under the trance. If any paper was gone be exchanged, they were gonna be on the receiving end.

So, I'm sitting there at the feet of Jayne, taking in all of her up-from-the-ghetto-girl superstar wisdom when we notice an admirer.

"Girl that clown wit da bow tie like you. Don't talk to him, he think he a pimp."

"Ain't no harm in talkin."

"That nigga useta be the camera man up here. He finally talked up on some lil broad, now he be dressed all up pimp-style. He a simp."

"Well, since he a simp, he ain't dangerous." He winked at me and I gave him a smile, as he approached our table looking dead at me.

"How you doin baby?"

"Fine."

"You damn right about dat. You sho is fine. Can I get you some juice?"

"I'll take some cranberry juice."

"Cool, let me go get dat fa you. I'll be right back." As he stepped away, Jayne began her lecture.

"Fuck him and feed him dogshit. If you like him and wanna hook up wit him, make him take you out. Never leave wit a nigga that you didn't come with. That makes a nigga think you easy. You want respect. He might be able to get otha broads to do dis an' nat but let him know you ain't no any broad. I wish a muthafucka would step to me wit dat slick shit. Be careful cause dese niggas is full a game."

I heard everything Jayne said. But everything she said attracted me to him even more. A couple guys in high school tried to holla at me, but I never liked them. They were corny. I liked brothas that didn't quite walk or talk straight. Deep inside, I didn't think a "decent" college guy or a square guy could like me. When I shared with Andrew that I got raped and had an abortion, he didn't pamper me or attempt to make that painful experience up to me. He taught me how to be a "bottom woman"—a hardcore, stand-by-yo-man chick. I sat there eagerly awaiting AC's return with my juice. I wanted to hear every little thing he had to say:

"Do you mind if we find a more intimate place to sit?"

"No," I said.

"That's my lil cousin, so wherever you take her, make sho she come back here," Jayne said with a smirk on her face and in her voice.

AC smiled a devilish smile, took me by the hand and held it as we found an empty stool at the end of the bar in another room. He sat me down there, with my back to the bar. He stood close to me to intoxicate me with the smell of his cologne. And it was workin.

"What you up to up in here?"

"Just hangin out wit my girls."

"I like you. I noticed you soon as you came in here. You got them big ole legs and nem sexy big lips."

"Thank you. You pretty sexy yoself."

"A lotta niggas be leapin and fallin all over dem twins cause they redbones and shit. Gimme the sexy brown sister any day."

"Ain't nobody said nuthin bout givin nobody to nobody yet."

"Not yet. I don't want nobody dat don't want me. If you gimme a chance, I'ma tell ya like the Supremes, 'I'm gonna make you love me.'"

"We talkin bout love and we barely in like."

"I can take care of all dat. Where you spendin the rest of the night?"

"Hangin out wit my girls."

"What y'all wanna do?"

"Let's find out." I made my way over to the other room and back to our original table. Jayne was gone but Diamond and Jean were still there all up in each other's faces.

"Where Jayne?"

"See her over dere talking to Hubert, the fur man," Jean explained.

"Well, what we gon' do when we leave here?"

"We gone go over Jayne's for some drinks and whutnot. She got seafood, ribs and shit and Diamond got the caine."

"I'ma ask AC if he wanna come, too, is that cool?"

"Cool."

Jayne waved me over to her. She introduced me to Hubert as the man that had the best deals in the city on mink coats, fur jackets, hats and ladies clothing. I traded Black love hugs with him and let Jayne know that AC would be coming with us. She said she was alright with it.

We met up in Vincent's parking lot so that AC and Diamond could follow us in their cars to Jayne's.

Jayne's interior decorator skills were on full display. Her place was sharp and I took pride in it as though it was mine. We gathered in her living room. Jean put on some music, while Jayne looked after the food. Diamond cleared off a space on the cocktail table for cocaine which he began shaping into lines and snorting:

"Hey man, git down."

"Naw, man I pass," AC said.

"What about your lady friend?"

"If she fuck wit dat, I don't want her." AC looked me in the eye and asked, "You drink and drug?"

"Not really."

"Good, that shit is for suckahs."

Diamond shoots back, "Suckahs lose control. Real niggas don't let nuthin control dem."

"Whatevah, man."

Jayne called us into the dining room for food. After we had a bite to eat, AC and I remained at the dining table while everyone else went back to the living room. That night, AC gave me his full attention and I gave him mine. Like most people that I know who have served time, AC explained that he had been wrongfully convicted, that he had done a 4-year bid for aggravated assault. He said that he was married and divorced. That he didn't have no love for his ex-wife, but that he kept it civil with her because he loved their daughter. When I pressed him for details about his marriage, he just said that his ex wasn't good for him and he wasn't good for her. That she was holding him back in life.

Well, who was I to judge? My past wasn't squeaky clean, but I didn't want AC to know it. I told him that I attended Cleveland State University and that I worked part time at Cleveland Trust bank as a proof operator. I didn't want him to know that I lived and grew up on East 68th and Cedar because people judged you differently when they knew that. And I certainly didn't want him to know that I had worked as a prostitute, a car tamperer, that I had been a street-hustla's "bottom woman."

"What are you taking up in college?"

I didn't have any focus and I wasn't giving my studies full attention. Plus, I was still in Special Studies, Student Support Services, which I thought made me look dumb. So I just answered:

"Law."

"I cain't knock dat."

AC explained that he was a PK (preacher's kid), that he had grown up in the Lee-Harvard area and had graduated from John

F. Kennedy. Like I said, JFK people always thought they were better than us, down in the hood, East Tech scarabs, so I was glad that I didn't mention Cedar. But the more and more we talked I could see that AC didn't seem that proud of his upbringing. He was proud that he had boxed in the penitentiary. He was all about fitness and health and kept complimenting me on my physique, my "big ole legs" and my behind. We talked, or should I say, he talked, until the break of dawn. He offered to take me home but I refused because I was staying over with Jayne. We exchanged numbers and agreed that he would pick me up later that evening.

AC had an Evander Holyfield body. About the height and weight of Holyfield. A good-looking brotha, he wore his hair parted down the middle. He had nice soft looking lips and beautiful white teeth—one of his fronts was gold. He arrived in a warm-up suit. I was dressed up. He said we would just spend a quiet evening at his humble abode. *Okay*, I thought. *At least he knows how I roll.* We drove across town to 93rd off of Cedar Avenue! This is my hood. I knew Cedar like the back of my hand, from the 30th Street projects all the way to 105th St. He lived on the top floor of a two-story apartment building that his parents owned. He didn't have any furniture except a bed, a dresser, some weights and a television in his bedroom, and a stove and refrigerator in the kitchen. He was roughing it. We sat on his bed and talked for a long while. After some time, he asked if I was going to take off my clothes.

"I wadn't plannin on it."

He held my face in his two hands and kissed my lips. He drew circles around my eyes and my nose, studying my anatomy.

"You got a white people nose."

"Yeah, my Daddy useta to make us push the bridges of our noses up every morning. That was our routine. Get up, wash up, put on noxema and shape our noses before…"

Before I could finish he stuck his tongue in my mouth, tasting my lips, alternating between my lips and my neck as his hands searched for zippers, snaps, buttons to undo to get rid of any piece of clothing standing between him and my body. I started helping him with my clothes. He got up, took off his and got on top of me. AC was a straight up type of dude. He didn't like anything kinky. I was glad. To be honest, it wasn't anything to write home about. No disrespect to him. He had all the right equipment. Maybe it was just me. Maybe it's because I got a raw deal with my first sexual experience. Or, maybe it was Andrew teaching me how to have oral sex with him. Or, maybe it was because Candy taught me about acting when turning tricks. Whatever it was, sex just wasn't all that to me. I never really got that much out of it. I just did it because it was expected.

I was working at Cleveland Trust, "going to school," partying, and hanging out with AC. My grades were not good. I had no focus. I had a 1.9 GPA. Two of the classes that I took were Art History and Introduction to Physics. I was supposed to be writing a term paper for the Art History course and I had checked all of these books out of the library and never opened them. I had reverted to my junior high school model, where I could show up for class whenever I wanted and still get at least a C. My mindset was "just do enough to pass." But college was different. You had to attend classes consistently, participate and study. Needless to say, I neglected to do any of these. I hardly read course materials, but I did take notes when I went to class.

I did most of the assignments, except the final paper in Art History class. In the Physics class, there were mostly no-credit homework assignments that were supposed to get you ready for the midterm. The Physics professor gave a lot of lectures. I hardly heard any of them. I remember the professor tapping me on the shoulder quite a few days to wake me up from a good slob on your sleeve snooze. I failed the midterm. My only hope of passing was to ace the final. I decided I was gonna do it. I crammed one weekend and I got an A on the final and a C in the class. But it wasn't enough to thwart that fateful day—too many dropped courses, too many incompletes, too low of a GPA—the day of academic dismissal. Well, you know what they say: "When one door closes another one opens." I told myself that I didn't care, that I could always go back to school later.

By this time, I had bought a few pieces of furniture that I stored in my parents' basement, and I was planning to move out on my own. AC began picking me up from work evenings at Cleveland Trust. We mostly rode around the strolls on Cedar, Prospect and Euclid. Sisters that worked on these strolls were fly. They looked like movie stars. Long wigs, high heels, long eyelashes, sparkly jewelry, made-up faces, flashy sexy outfits, fur jackets. I always liked street people. I know it sounds crazy and I can't explain it, but there is a certain honesty there. And I totally loved the ambiance of the night life on nights when the block rocked with action. Bright lights, sexy voices and sexy legs and arms directing traffic—estrogen extravaganza! "Hey baby," "Spend some money honey," "Wanna date?" "Let's have some fun." Walkin and workin it.

All AC talked about was how much he loved hoes. He always said "Ain't nuthin in this world betta than a thoroughbred hoe." When we weren't out cruising the strolls, we'd ride through one of his friends' cribs. Two of AC's best friends were "retired" pimps—Ralph and Bow Leg. AC really respected both of these guys. All they kicked was pimpology. How many hoes, homes, businesses, cars. How many White girls; how well-respected a pimp was nationally. If a pimp wasn't nationally known, he was seen as poot-butt. AC didn't have a rep as a pimp. He was known for "knockin niggas out in the penitentiary." But he wanted to be a pimp—extra super bad.

He had a bad attitude and a chip on his shoulder because his status wasn't hood. After I got to see how he interacted with his parents, I could see that he resented them. (I resented my parents too, but for other reasons—for not making me pretty, for not being rich, for being old, and for being different).

One day, after we had been together for a while, his mother noticed that I had been beaten. He got angry and called his mother a bitch. If I didn't leave him after the beating, I sho nuff shoulda left after he called his mother a bitch. I was a rotten apple, and I had been around some rotten apples, but I had never heard anybody call they momma a bitch! The brother had issues.

AC also suffered from that age old Black disease—I'm As Black As You—or the Blacker Than Thou. You know, that disease that forces you to prove to your peers that you ain't no lame just because you didn't grow up in stereotypical poor Black circumstances. He grew up in the Lee-Harvard area, which was at the time, a middle-class Black neighborhood. The stereotypical roughnecks came out of the projects—Central, Cedar, King Kennedy, Morris Black, Outhwaite—or they were off of Hough, Wade Park, Superior, St. Clair among other known hoods. But to be sure, Lee-Harvard didn't have a rep. AC could box his butt off. Everywhere we went, he got his propers. Not because brothers liked him, but because they knew they would have to blow his brains out. In AC's mind, he was the ultimate Black man. He could tolerate nothing less, especially homosexuals. One day, we were walking down Euclid in downtown Cleveland and this guy greeted him:

"Hey man, what's happenin?" "How you been doing?" The guy smiles and holds out his hand for AC to shake. What did he do that for? AC starts spitting wildly just barely missing the guy's face.

"You bitch-ass, faggot-ass nigga. You sucked dick in the penitentiary and you gon' try to speak to me? I wouldn't shake yo dick holdin hand! Nigga if you see me, cross the muthafuckin street before I crack yo muthafuckin head, you nasty-ass bitch-ass nigga. You got dat?"

By this time, AC and this poor guy were face to face and the guy's face is covered in AC's spit.

"Yeah, man. I got it."

In my twisted logic, I needed AC on my arm, just as much as he needed me on his. AC was all about stacking paper. He talked about money. How to save. He'd always say, it's not how much money a hoe makes, it's about how much a man don't waste. AC didn't get high, so I knew whatever money I made wouldn't be wasted on dope. Plus, his sobriety was good for me and delayed the onset of my full-blown alcoholism and drug addiction. While I was with AC, the strongest drink to pass through these lips was Pepsi-Cola, and the only thing I smoked was Newports. Another reason I liked being with AC was he didn't have any other women when I met him. Although I had heard that he had one other broad before me, she wasn't around when I came on the scene.

Most of all, AC didn't really know my hood status. Afterall, when we first met, he only knew me as a college girl. He didn't know my total M.O. If he was able to "turn me out" that would solidify his status as a bonafide playa. Little did he know, I was hardly a turnout. I let him think that I was a totally square broad. From the time I was young, I noticed that a lot of men didn't respect and protect sistas from da hood, just on GP. I wanted the fact of my being a college girl to outshadow my hoodness. Good girls don't do this and bad girls do that. Good girls look like this and not that. Bad girls are from here and not there.

Once I became a full-time streetgirl so many so-called "decent" men would always say "Why are you out here? You seem like a nice girl. Why don't you get out of this life before you get killed or hurt?" or "Ain't no decent man gonna want you if you stay out here too long." "You don't wanna get old out here. This life is for young girls. What you gonna do when you get older?" Funny thing about the decent man thing is that the same ones, who were asking me why I was out there selling, were the same ones out there buying. Preachers, teachers, police officers, steel mill workers, auto workers, business men—all types of men (most of them married). Most of these "decent" hard-working men worked at J & L Steel, Ford, Chrysler, The City of Cleveland etc. One thing is for sure, I felt more comfortable around playas and hustlas like AC. They were less hypocritical. Plus, street guys liked me, or at least that's what I thought.

This was the late 1970s, before crack hit the streets of Cleveland. When I agreed to work for AC, I began working on the Cedar Avenue stroll, a stroll that was right down the street from my neighborhood. When I was with Drew, we worked on what I would later find out were "lower ranked" strolls, where "faggs," transvestites, and drug addicts worked. But AC had to have me "kick the bricks" with the girls and the playas who were known to be "top flight," and such folks worked on Cedar, Prospect, 40th and Euclid, in go-go spots, and major chain hotels. I had become one of the glamour girls that I so admired.

My first night out, I was nervous because you had to be strong. I knew that from being with Drew, plus AC kept drilling me. You couldn't let nobody know that you were afraid of nothing. You had to walk out there alongside the traffic and flag guys over in a way that did not cause you to bump heads with another girl. If for some reason you did, you had to be ready to throw down and defend yourself, especially if you and your man were unknown. AC lived right around the corner from the main strip, so he walked me out. This served the purpose of letting everybody know, I was his bitch. Girls that didn't have male representation could not work without huge problems. She would be labeled as a renegade and would be seen as putting herself on the level of a man.

For this reason, "bulldaggers" who had their own hoes and who did not have men were hated by playas. But I was out there. AC left. He had to leave me on my own to prove to his peers that his game was tight. He'd schooled me about how to handle myself, how to clock dollas, and stay alive. Every step I took marked my territory and my status as a down-ass hoe. As I began to stroll and flag cars, this one girl kept checking me out. I mean she was doing some serious scoping. Finally, she called to me "Is that you Big Stuff?" I recognized that voice right away, but the frame was all different. It was my girl, Candy, from back in the day, about 100 pounds heavier.

"What's up bitch? Where you been? What happened to yo nigga Drew? I see my glamour lessons paid off. You look like money."

"Girl, I ain't wit Drew no more. I'm wit this nigga AC now. Don't mention to nobody how you know me. This nigga think I'ma turnout."

"You ole crusty hoe. Shit, turnout. If you a turnout, I'm a virgin."

"You still wit Fox?"

"Girl, Fox got killed. I can't even talk about it right now. I been wit dis nigga Skillet for the last coupla years. I don't love him. Me and him ain't tight like me and Fox was. He got a lot of otha hoes and a White transvestite. The only reason why I'm wit him is cause he don't press me bout makin no quota. If I hit a lick, I give him what I want to give him. He knows I got a kid and I still send money home every week. I gained all this damn weight when Fox died. Fat bitches don't make much money in the hotels. Thass why I start workin out here full time. If it wasn't for my baby, I wouldn't care about nuthin. But a bitch still be hittin licks now. You know. It ain't a bitch in this town can outsteal me. We can work togetha sometimes cause I don't even deal wit my wife-in-laws. Skanks."

"Girl, I gotta git busy foe dis nigga catch me out here fellowshippin. We'uh link up, hear?"

We hugged and went on about our business. This was definitely a different type of stroll. AC would dart in and out to check my trap kinda regularly. Seems like every other trick I caught, he was right there to collect the money. Other playas would keep ridin up and down the track to advertise themselves, to see if any new fish was on the block, and to see if any renegades or unknowns were around.

Pimps pursued turnouts mercilessly. One pimp named Roses tried his best to win me over to his stable. He kept hollerin:

"Hey sexy mama. I know you want a real pimp in yo life. A man you can see the world with. A man who get his propers from Maine to Miami. A man that know how to work wit everythang you got. That's what you need. You on't need a wannabee. You need a man that can show you how to get some real money, so when you too old to sell pussy, you can retire wit yo own bidnesses. That's what Ahm about baby. Only a dumb bitch a pass a playa like me up. Come on home baby."

I walked away from him and tried to stay out of earshot but he was determined to make me hear every word he was saying. I looked silly walking and trotting trying not to listen to him. I knew AC was ridin and checkin on me. He told me many times what to expect from other pimps. It was their job to try to knock me off and it was my job to ignore them, not look them in their faces and not ever smile.

AC lived in a house that his parents owned, so his overhead was low. Plus, it was right around the corner. He approached pimping systematically. As I said earlier, he didn't drink, smoke or get high. He was about stacking money. He had studied the Cedar stroll. He knew when the block was hot. When money was on the street. AC taught me to socialize but to keep it focused on watching out for the rollers, the vice squad, kidnappers and stick up boys. Almost every dime I gave him, he put in a suitcase under his bed. I was becoming known as a bitch that was strickly bout bizness. It was a balancing act. A girl had to be friendly enough with other girls so that they would tell you if something was going down and at the same time make them respect you.

Now, I should mention that I was still working at Cleveland Trust. My job was working on a machine that looked like a giant calculator except that you punched in check amounts and they had to balance to a deposit slip. Needless to say, my attendance was starting to suffer. It was time for me to move out of my parents' house. It was only a matter of time before they would find out about me. I decided it was time to quit my job at Cleveland Trust and became a full time employee for AC. Of course AC encouraged me along these lines but it wasn't his fault. When you hate yourself, that's the kind of stuff you do. AC and I sneaked all of my furniture out of my parents' basement one day, and we were totally together.

•7•

The Death of AC and the Birth of My Drug Habit

AC DIDN'T HAVE MANY friends, but the ones he had he cherished. He loved the ground Boe Leg hobbled on. Boe was a father figure. He was a dark-skinned, extra skinny man, with a drawn face and teeth that way too much caffeine and nicotine had passed through. You could look into Boe's eyes and know that he'd seen a lot of things in this world. Whatever he had gone through, he managed to keep a smile on his face and a warm personality. Boe had been a pimp in his younger days, but now, he was a junkie. AC wouldn't normally befriend a dope fiend, but Boe never got high around AC, and more important than that, Boe was a walking encyclopedia of the game in Cleveland and NYC, his two stomping grounds.

AC loved to listen to Boe tell him all about his life history in pimpdom. So, they were real cool. Boe had a White girl, who was also a junkie. Her name was Joan. She had been shot in the back by a trick. Although the shooting left her physically challenged and walking with a cane, she still would work on the White girl stroll. She had to pay for her drugs somehow. Boe had apartments in both NYC and Cleveland and he traveled between them often. AC was fascinated by all the accounts of the pimp-ho game in NYC and he was dying to go. In order to be classified as a true national playa, you had to work yo broad in NYC. Boe is the person that took us to NYC and turned AC on to the NYC strolls.

When we got to Boe's NYC crib, and I do mean crib, I was surprised by the number of people who slept there each night. Boe rented out the bathtub (one person slept there), the kitchen floor (two people), the couch (where AC and I slept). Sometimes he rented the bathroom floor too. The only space he didn't rent out was the bedroom where he slept with Joan. During the day, Boe drove us around NYC showing us where the nightspots were. I should just say spots, because many of them were 100% active in the daytime, too. Now if I thought the Cleveland strolls were swift, multiply that times 100, and you'd have the pace of the NYC strolls. This was the city that never slept. And AC wanted me to keep pace.

The action that was popping on the 39th and 11th Avenue stroll gave a whole new meaning to "broad daylight." All kinds of girls worked this track—Puerto Rican, White, Black. They came from down south, across country. You name it. Wall to wall girls out there, strolling like they owned the place. Girls were pulling over cars, trucks, vans, motorcycles, sometimes bikers and walkers. Sometimes 2 or 3 girls would be working one vehicle. On this stroll nobody went below the belt-all money was made with breasts, hands, lips and condoms. Each girl's objective: accumulating bank by emptying as many wallets as possible, 5 minutes or less per pop. The method on this stroll was to pull over a vehicle right on the spot. Get a guy to roll his window all the way down and give up some money, talk dirty and use your hands and breasts until he spent every dollar.

Last resort was to actually open the guy's door and give a blow job. This caused problems sometimes because a lot of the tricks would want to do something else or go somewhere else and felt ripped off. Many a girl could be seen jumping out of moving vehicles. Since this was a drive through stroll, walkers were always suspected of being stick-up cats, so a girl had to always be on the look out.

The next thing I knew AC come lookin at me talkin about "Sexy, go on out there and see what you can do." Now Mama woulda said with that you ought to be ashamed but ain't look— "dem shame chree dead." But my shame tree wasn't dead yet and I wasn't too keen on working in the daytime. I still had a twig of shame left in my game. I looked at AC like he was crazy.

"I ain't workin out dere," I frowned.

AC opened Boe's car door:

"Gon' and see what you can do. We uh be back." He said very matter of factly.

"Ugghh," I murmured as I slowly moved out of Boe's car. As I approached the thick of the action, I adjusted the snap in my step to match the swift money making flow and vibe of the area. After a few failed attempts to get some money, I realized that my best bet was to be the first girl at a car because a lot of these girls were wife-in-laws and worked in teams, so they weren't about to share a car with a non-family member.

"Okay," I said to myself. "I see how y'all gon' roll." I moved to what I thought was an ideal location and began to get first dibbs on vehicles. I hit a streak. Before I knew anything I had turned about 8 or 9 tricks. But I was still glad to see AC and Boe come back through because I didn't know who was counting how many tricks I turned to rob me, and I feared some guy was gonna try to pull off with me and I'd have to leap out of a racing vehicle and get all scarred up or worse. When Boe and AC pulled up, I jumped in the car and pulled out a wad of cash from under my wig. AC shoved it into his pocket, saying "We uh come back through here later on tonight." Little did I know that that night would be my first in jail.

When we came back at dusk the block wasn't poppin as it did earlier and there seemed to be a different crew of girls out there. I had a bad feeling, but I tried to throw it out of my mind and just get on with the night. As soon as I stepped foot on the track, the first car I solicited was a decoy. He pulled over, played the little game with me but wouldn't unzip his pants and insisted that I get in the car. As soon as I hopped in and asked for money, he reached under his leg and came up with some handcuffs and cuffed me, while another officer came and walked me to an undercover van containing a bunch of other girls.

We were like so many sheep being led to slaughter. First, they took us to what amounts to a large holding pen, where we were interviewed, then strip searched—They took our cigarettes, purse, everything. Then allowed us to make one phone call. I didn't have a number to call. No one had cell phones back then and Boe Leg didn't have a "house" phone. We moved around all night, it seems, from precinct to precinct, picking up arrested girls all the way, until we got to our final destination—100 Centre Street. Thank goodness, Boe knew the ropes and when I was arraigned the next day, Boe and AC were there to bail me out. When I got out, AC and Boe congratulated me on surviving my first arrest.

The thing I hated about getting busted was that all that effort put into accumulating money is negated because you have to give it back to post bail and pay lawyers. It's like selling your soul for free! But this is the life of street people. Some days are good and some days you go to jail.

After getting out of jail, it was time to make up for lost revenue. AC and Boe had been scoping out another stroll on 38th and 8th Avenue. This was a walk-up stroll where girls took their tricks into a hotel on 38th Street. You had to work within the flow of pedestrian traffic and try to make eye contact with men, to persuade them to spend some money, without being too obvious so that business owners wouldn't call the police. This, too, was a broad daylight and anytime of night stroll. It was a little safer because you didn't have to get into a car for any reason. This became my favorite NYC stroll.

I learned just enough Spanish to solicit Spanish-speaking tricks: "Tu queres salir?" I code-switched on All-American White boys on vacation: "Hey babe, let's party." And I abided by the rule Fat Bitch taught me: neva sell to a young nigga. Using these practices along with charging in five-minute intervals, I began to make what we called White girl money. In Cleveland, a good night for a flatbacking Black girl on the stroll was 5 to 6 hundred dollars on a weekend, 2 to 3 hundred on a weeknight. But on this block, I was clocking 2 to 3 hundred dollars every 2 to 3 hours. Most of the tricks didn't give any problems; but every now and then drama would jump off.

The first time I saw a girl get seriously hurt in NYC was on 8th Avenue not far from the Port Authority. Some trick sliced this girl's face wide open. Apparently, he had been ripped off—I don't know if she was the one who did it, but he took his revenge on her. She came flying out of the transit hotel flailing about, like a chicken with its head off, except her head was on and she was screaming and whaling—"look at my face!" The red blood gushed from her face from a long, large open gap. She had friends or wife-in-laws who ran over to console her—some of them ran into the transit hotel to see if they could find the guy who did it.

Apparently, he had already escaped. The injured girl and some attendants sat on the sidewalk until an ambulance came.

But the beat went on. Girls were steadily catching tricks as I watched in horror. AC always told me that world class hoes can read a trick's face and know whether or not he was gonna give trouble. For that reason, I always tried to hold a dialogue with a potential client, long enough to see if his face would tell me whether or not he would hurt me. Of course, that method was not fool proof. Fools come in all races, sizes and dispositions. I worked in NYC for about a month on that first trip. My final stay was at Riker's Island, where I finished a 10 day sentence.

In Riker's you meet girls from all over the country. It's where you hear all the gossip. Girls bragged on their men, how long they'd been with a guy, if they had a baby for him, how good or bad a guy treated his women, how much jewelry, clothes, cars they owned. Another big topic was which girls got paid top dollar and White girl money. What kind of business the girl was gonna have when she retired. Some girls would try to convince other girls to leave their current pimp and join their family. Some girls from large families with a lot of girls were competing against each other for the bottom woman spot. The girl who brought home another girl from jail and got them to choose her man earned thoroughbred points and status within the family. I was never the type that wanted to share my guy so I wasn't listening and I certainly wasn't soliciting no broad to come home with me and AC. A lot of girls traveled all over the country and they exchanged info about the country's best strolls.

Another thing we did to pass the time was sing along with the radio. Some girls would start crying on the "quiet storm" when touching love songs came on. Some girls were estranged from their biological families and hadn't seen them in years. Sometimes we'd dance together on party music, braid each other's hair or just plain ole shit-talk to pass the time.

On the day of my release, which was also our last day in NYC before returning to Cleveland, AC and I went shopping. He picked me out a couple leather jackets, a few leather mini-skirts, some tops, some heels, a new wig, some jewelry and cologne. He got himself a gold chain with diamonds and a letter A.

The first thing AC did when we got back to Cleveland was buy a pimpmobile. His choice was a Lincoln Towncar, white interior, soft leather seats, white top, metallic green exterior. It wasn't brand new, but it was new enough to be really nice and clean. Now that he had the car, the look, the credentials, we had to go to Vincent's to let all of our circle see how good we looked, how we were coming up in the world. There was some commotion at the door of Vincent's that night. We stood in line while the bodyguard at the door patted down men and searched women's purses for weapons. While we were standing in line, an argument broke out between two playas—House and this other dude, who seemed to come up missing after that night. I don't remember anything except the part when this playa, Roses, tried to calm the whole thing down by saying, "Man we all playas in here. This don't make no sense. Come on gentlemen." And with that, House reared back and bust Roses dead in the mouth, and said "Bitch, shut up when you see two men talkin." AC turned to me and said, "Every nigga that look the part, ain't it."

Just because Roses had women, dressed like a playa and hung out in all the right places, didn't mean he was respected. Street playas always tested each other's manhood and Roses came up weak. He was just standing there, trying to kick it. After that blow to the mouth, he just stood there, holding his lip, looking stupid. A couple bodyguards came over and put him out. After taking that bitch-slap and no come back, that was basically the end of his pimp career. News travels fast.

AC's new status as national playa preceded our return to Cleveland. When we stepped up in Vincent's, it seemed like all eyes were on us. We both looked like money, AC displaying his new chain with the giant diamond encrusted A, and me in one of my new leather git ups, looking like we were paid in the shade. AC led me over to a bar stool and beckoned to the barmaid as he spied a booth with some guys he admired. He ordered us cranberry and gingerale juice drinks and went to fellowship. I spotted Jayne and Jean and went over to their booth. When they looked up and saw me, they stopped their chatting in mid-sentence, as Jean grabbed me by the arm and sat me down.

"Uhm uhm uh," said Jayne in that Black girl head noddin rhythm we do. "I know this ain't Lainey, looking like a world-class hooker. Where you been?" She said asking a fake question she already knew the answer to.

"New York."

"Girl, I know you got you a new car to match that new outfit. Ain't no way in the hell I'ma help a nigga buy him a new ride and I ain't got one, too."

"I'ma get mine next," I said half embarrassed.

"Girl, you betta get yours," Jean butted in. "You shoulda got yours first. Memba Pat?"

"What Pat?"

"Pat that useta live on the corner of 70th and Cedar. Bad-ass body, Pat, wit da big ass that was wit dat nigga V," Jean explained.

"Yeah, what about her?"

"She dead. They found her ass in a trick house on 83rd and Cedar. Somebody shot her. They killin women out here like 40 going norf."

"And when they find a Black girl dead out here, don't nobody feel it, 'cept they momma. Dese niggas keep on rollin. They don't miss one beat. So you betta get yours first, if you gon' be out dere like dat. Shee-it. Know what uhm sayin?" Said Jayne.

AC was never too keen on Jayne and Jean because he knew they never liked the idea of me being with him. Jayne and Jean never looked down on me for prostituting, but they knew me ever since I was a little girl. They loved my family and they called my mother Auntie Evelyn. They were like family and they weren't feeling their little cousin being a hoe, especially giving the proceeds to a man. It seemed like as soon as we were getting down into the ins and outs of all I had seen in NYC, AC found me at our booth.

"What's up twins?" AC greeted Jayne and Jean.

"Hey AC," they replied in harmony.

"Well, we'uh be seeing y'all," AC said as he gave me the let's roll head nod command. I hugged Jayne and Jean and got up to follow AC out.

"Lainey, we love you baby. Don't forget whut we talked about. We love you baby." Said Jayne and Jean, as I walked away with AC.

AC didn't like the sound of our parting conversation:

"What dem out-of-order bitches want you to remember?"

"That I should be careful cause Pat got killed and girls be gitting killed all the time."

"Yeah, niggas was telling me about Pat. That broad was a dope fiend though. That's why she got killed. When ya mind ain't clear out here, you make wrong moves. That's why I don't fuck

with dope. You just listen to what I say and we gon' go to the top."
And so our conversation went as we left Vincent's, got in the car,
and began to ride toward Cedar:

"You gittin money tonight?"

Of course, I knew the question was really a command, so I
agreed and he dropped me off on the Cedar stroll. All the Cedar
thoroughbred Allstars were out that night: Queen Bee, Georgia,
Green Eyes, Big Niecey, Lil' Niecey, Big Cat. The block was
rocking, but best of all, who did I see again but my girl Candy.
She came right over to my work spot and a few minutes after we
exchanged greetings, *Boop. Boop. Boop. Bad ah, dah, dah dah!* A
barrage of gunshots went off. Everybody scattered. It happened so
fast my head was spinning. Candy threw her arm around the back
of my head, and pushed me down. "Stay down and move out!"

I was like, "What the hell?" As I heard a bullet sizzle past
my right ear, I almost peed up my new leather mini. My movie
star vibe went right out the window, as we dropped down to our
knees and crawled war-style on all fours, making our way behind
the gas station and through the field towards the transit house.
Candy was giggling her head off all the way like she had just
heard a good Richard Pryor joke: "Girl, I ripped this nigga's cash
out his wallet and I couldn't get the wallet back in his pants." I'm
thinking, *Lord how in the hell did I get in this movie!*

"Bitch, I'ma blow yo fuckin brains out if you don't gimme
back my wallet," hollered a furious trick.

See, Candy was getting scandalous. Every thieving hoe
knows, when you hit a lick, you never go back on the same corner.
You always change your look, different wig, clothes, different
location or just don't come back out for a few nights or maybe
even weeks depending on how much money was involved. Plus,
only rob White guys. They were much less likely to ride through

a Black stroll area trying to find the girl who ripped them off. But Candy had broken all these rules. *And* she was laughing while this guy was trying to blow her away. My emotions were running between mad as hell and scared to death.

We finally made it through the field and ran to the transit house door. Candy rang the bell repeatedly, and the owner let us in. Thank God, Candy and the house owner, Chuck, were good friends. He told us to go downstairs in the basement until things cooled off. Pretty soon, we heard the car pull into the driveway and the bell ring. Chuck went to the door and talked to the guy, assuring him that he didn't know anything about it and that no girls were there. Needless to say, I was traumatized. I wasn't going back out there that night. After I got through calling Candy every crazy ass bitch in the book, I decided to take my chances and walk through backyards on 93rd to get to me and AC's place. I made it there and stayed put until he came home.

I explained everything that happened, but he didn't want to hear it. He felt I should have stayed out that night and worked. Not to come home broke. He claimed that other girls were out there working up a storm when he rode through. I didn't give a damn who was out there. I wasn't going back out there. He cussed me out, calling me all kinds of "punk-ass bitches." I didn't say a word. He was gonna have to kill me that night. I stood my ground. I wasn't going back out that night. It was this incident and quite a few others like it that built up in me the courage to leave AC.

The Frankie incident was the worst. It started about AC bringing a broad home one day saying she was my new wife-in-law. Now, I had had a wife-in-law before when I was with Andrew, but

Andrew never tried to make us live together or be all up in each other's faces. I felt like I had invested my life enough with AC that he didn't have to bring his other broad up in my face. My view was "Okay, have your other chick, but she needs her own place. She ain't staying here." I felt like he just wanted her to stay with us so he could show off to his boys that he was 2 deep. I felt like he had already made a name off of me. How much more did he need to prove to his boys that he was a real pimp?

The next day, when he dropped me off to work, I was depressed. I stood there on the corner crying. One of AC's so-called friends, Frankie, saw me standing on the corner crying. And for a moment, I forgot that Frankie was a snake. Frankie invited me over his house, which was just down the street from the stroll and I went—like a dummy. He befriended me and told me to tell him everything that was wrong, come over and rest a while. He consoled me saying that he would talk to AC, that I was a good girl and AC should understand where I was coming from. He said, "You just sleep here tonight and tomorrow, I'll go talk to AC and everything will be alright."

Frankie treated me like a queen. He brought me food. Fixed up the couch real nice for me. Told me jokes to cheer me up. I really thought he was going to do what he said. The next day, he said, "I don't think you should go home today. AC gon' be mad cause you ain't called him. Wait another day until he cools off, and then I'll go talk to him for you." Frankie tells me to just stay put, that tomorrow would be a better day. I felt comfortable. I trusted he would help me. Later that night I am awakened by kisses on my legs. I jump up to Frankie looking in my eyes.

"Hey lady, everything's cool. I just wanna make you feel good."

"If I didn't know any better, I woulda thought you was tryna fuck me."

"Naw bitch, you tryna fuck me. You need to leave that clown-ass nigga. He ain't no real pimp. That nigga a camera man. He need you, you don't need him. You need to come on and be wit me."

"Oh, nah, Frankie. I don't wanna choose you. I thought you were AC's friend and that you were foreal. Just let me out of here. I want to go home."

"Bitch, the only way you gettin outta here is you gone choose me, or I'ma tell AC you over here, and he gone beat the shit outta you. Think about it and make the right choice."

I begged Frankie to just let me go home and that he must go get AC for me. He wouldn't do it. A little while later, Frankie told me to go in the bedroom, that AC was at the door and that he was going to go talk to him. I hoped he would defend me to AC and tell him the truth.

The next thing I know, AC kicked in Frankie's bedroom door dragged me down Frankie's stairs, kicking me, punching me, all the way to his car. I was every "dumb no good bitch" in the book. He beat me so bad, I had two black eyes, a fat lip, lumps in my head and I was just bruised and sore all over my whole body. I wanted him to kill me, because I didn't think my life could go down any further. AC took me back to his place. My wife-in-law, Tina, ran a hot bath for me and put me in it.

"Damn girl, why you run off? He been ridin and lookin for you two days. Then he got word that you chose Frankie. What happened?"

I didn't answer. I hurt too bad, mentally and physically, to talk. I just sat there in the water wishing I was dead as she poured Epson Salt and alcohol in the water and bathed me. I only came out of the bedroom to go to the bathroom and I ain't say nothing to nobody for a few days. They'd bring me food and drink and they'd check on me. AC's parents came over one day while I was still in recovery. AC's mother came into the bedroom to look for me as though she knew about the beating. When she saw my face, she asked me if AC did it to me. I shook my head in agreement. She walked swiftly into the room where her husband was and told him "He's beating that nice girl, who moved all of this nice furniture in this place and is helping him." That's when AC said to his father, "Get yo bitch in check. Tell her to stay outta my bidness." I got up and ran to the bedroom door as AC and his father argued.

"Boy, what is wrong with you. What kind of beast is inside you to make you talk to us like this? And you round here beating on women that are nice to you."

"I run my bidness. You run yours ole man. Tell yo bitch to mind her own bidness."

"This is my house. You pack your things and get out."

"I'll get outta this shack. Just give me a few weeks and y'all can have this dump."

AC's poor mother and father. Mr. Wright had already had a stroke and walked with a cane. Mrs. Wright just stood there begging her husband to leave, saying that AC was gonna make him have a stroke or a heart attack. Finally, she convinced her husband to leave. As they were leaving, she turned to me and said, "Get away from him before he kills you."

I wanted to go home to my parents, but I was too ashamed. I felt that everybody in Cleveland now knew that I was a hoe. I would later find out that my family called the police on me constantly. They would have friends, Jayne and Jean among them, ride pass the stroll and try to spot me out. If they saw me, they would call the police. It seemed that I went to jail at least twice a week. I stayed with AC for a few more months, biding my time until I figured out how I was gonna leave him for good. I was glad that he had someone else, so I wouldn't have to leave him with no income. I didn't care about my furniture. I just wanted out, and I finally mustered up the nerve to go back home. When I did, my brother came to the door. When he saw me, he went back and told my father it was me. My father came and looked at me and closed the curtains. They didn't want to let me in. I stood at the door for what was only a few moments, but seemed like hours.

Finally, Mama came to the door: "This my dawta. Let her in."

When I came in the house, Mama hugged me and asked me if I was hungry. She didn't lecture me or ask me anything. She just left me alone. I went to bed and slept for what seemed like two weeks straight.

I went back to work, but this time, I was working a square job through the temp agency, and I started partying once again. Now I was doing a lot of hanging in my hood, and I ran around alot with one of my homeboys, Mugsy, and his girl. We went to neighborhood after-hour joints almost every weekend. Mugsy knew a lot of folks, and some of the spots we went to were drug spots. There were always 4 or 5 people going in the bathroom together. I didn't really know what kind of drugs they did, but I do know that whenever they came out of the bathroom, they looked and acted a lot different than they did before they went in. This got to be my crowd. They were always about to get high or just finishing getting high. I used to laugh at them, "Y'all act like y'all need that stuff."

One day Mugsy introduced me to one of his homeboys, Snap. Now, at this point in my life, I was not trying to be with a pimp, so Snap was cool. He was a nice guy to hang out with and he worked a square job. We started off just going out together. One thing led to another, and we became a couple. I still wasn't a big weed smoker or hardcore drinker. I just got buzzed. I graduated from Pink Champale to Miller's to Colt 45 and Old English 800, but I could take it or leave it. Eventually, I found out Snap shot drugs. I couldn't believe it. He didn't look bad and he was such a nice guy. He said he would never put a needle in my arm, that if I wanted to try it, that would be on me.

When he wasn't around one day, I asked one of the guys, Lil' G, to fix me up a shot. At the time, everybody was shooting these pills called T's & B's. Lil' G had no problem with it. He cooked up my shot and injected it in my arm. The rush was unbelievable. I never forgot that feeling. It felt warm. It rushed to the back of your throat down to your private parts to your feet. It was waaay better than sex, which as I stated earlier I never got that much out of anyway at that point in time. But I wasn't hooked instantly, or at least I didn't think so. At the time, I could take it or leave it. I was "a recreational drug user." But the crowd I rolled with lived to get high and it was only a matter of time. I had been with Snap for a few months just enjoying partyin and chillin.

One day when I got home, Mama said that AC's mother had been calling me and that I should call her right away. Now, I wasn't trying to hear anything from AC. In fact, I purposefully avoided being anywhere where there was even a slight chance that I would run into him. So I wondered why Mrs. Wright would be calling me. I was anxious to find out what was up so I rushed to return Mrs. Wright's call:

"Hi, Mrs. Wright, this is Elaine, AC's friend. My mom said that you called. How are you?"

"Honey, AC is dead."

"Oh, my God. Oh my God!"

"Yeah, he's gone, baby. He and some fellow had a disagreement in the Kinsman Chill and the guy shot him, honey. He's gone."

"Oh, Lord, Mrs. Wright. How are you? Ahm soooo sorry."

"Well, baby, I don't know how I am. I just knew something terrible was gonna happen to my son. I don't know what happened to my son. I know that you loved my son and that you bought that furniture in the apartment and I wanted you to get it and anything else you want from that apartment."

"Noooo, Mrs. Wright. I don't want anything."

I didn't want anything to remind me of nothing! I told her no. Mrs. Wright told me to call her the next day and she would give me the funeral arrangements. I had to find out the story on AC, so I had Snap ride me up on Cedar because I knew word would be on the street. My girls told me what went down.

AC's girl had beef with another girl and got sliced across the face. We used to call that Hoe Bidness and men didn't usually interfere, but AC was furious and went to the Kinsman Chill to check this playa about his woman. Now, the Kinsman Chill was this playa's spot. AC was usually a calculating type of guy, but he was so furious that his girl got cut, that all logic went out the window and he went up in another man's territory by himself. All of these were sucker moves. Word had it that AC got up in this man's face, put his gun all in his mouth and told him that no one beats his girl but him. The biggest sucker move AC made though was to put his gun away and turn his back. As soon as he turned to walk away, the back of his head was blown off.

The man had witnesses that said they saw AC put a gun in his mouth, and a gun was found on AC's body when the policed arrived. I don't know if Mrs. Wright ever heard the street version of her son's murder. The next day I called Mrs. Wright to get the funeral arrangements. I went to AC's funeral, but I didn't look in the casket. No one did any time for his murder, from what I heard.

•8•
Slammin Cadillac Do's

SNAP AND I WERE BAD for each other. He had no discipline and neither did I. Being away from AC gave me a new kind of freedom to wreck my life, my way. Not knowing what I wanted out of life, I existed day to day with no direction. My dream of being somebody was so far in the back of my mind I forgot it was there. All I cared about was having a "good time." Snap was in the same state of mind. He called in to his job one time too many and they told him he didn't have to worry about coming back. He was living with his grandma near East Cleveland, and since he was real good about helping her out with handyman chores and anything she needed, she wouldn't kick him out.

Snap's grandma was a staunch Christian. Her eyes said "I am endowed with Moses's authority to bust you over the head with these stone 10 Commandments. So if you ain't trying to help my boy get off dope and get right wit God, don't come round here!" I tried my best not to make eye contact with her cause her gaze went through my spirit. When I visited Snap at his grandma's I would just start immediately looking for chores. I'd start washing dishes, taking out trash, pulling weeds in the front yard—anything

Snap and me around 1979

to keep her from looking me in the eye. I was usually dressed in casual office attire. At the time, I still had my job through the temp agency and I was living at my parents' house, so my cover up game was still believable. I could even fool myself that I wasn't that bad off. After all, I could point to so many other people who were "way worse than me." It's so much easier to look down than it is to look up.

Snap and I got into a pattern of shootin up until we almost overdosed every Friday on my paydays. We called it "shootin the lights out." I'd cash my check on my lunch hour and give it to Snap to flip for me. We would put our money with others so we could buy a larger quantity. That way Snap and I had some to sell and some to use and I could make my paycheck money back. So, while I would be finishing out my Friday shift, Snap would go down to King's Bar on 55th near Cedar, make the deal and sell to customers who came through to cop. King's Bar was a haven for junkies, low-level drug dealers, and drag queens. So many drag queens hung out and lived in the upstairs apartments that people nicknamed it Queen's Bar. But King's was such a busy drug trafficking spot that usually by the time I got off work, Snap would have our drugs ready, my cash back and a couple hundred bucks for himself. We would get a hotel room for the weekend at Lancie's Motel on Carnegie and "shoot the lights out." One reason Lancie's was so popular was because of its location.

Map of Cleveland inner city neighborhood and stroll area

Carnegie Avenue, like Chester Avenue, offered a stream of potential middle- to upper-class customers to street hustlers during rush hours. Eastern suburbs began not too far east of East 105th Street.

The City of Cleveland set traffic lights and speed limits up so that surburbanites could flow through the hood and into downtown Cleveland to work without too many stops. Street hustlers would stroll around the corners of Chester, Carnegie, and Euclid hoping to stir up some curiosity and business. Street walkers and pimps liked Lancie because it was in the heart of the city, close to hoe strolls and after-hours spots, and the rent was cheap. A lot of playas kept a room there so they could rest their women or themselves between shifts. Dope dealers and users also liked Lancie. It was a good meeting spot. In front of the motel, Lancie's well-known restaurant faced Carnegie. Lancie ran neck to neck with Mark's Seafood for the best fish dinners in the city. The irony of Lancie's Steak House was that some of everybody came through. The lunch and happy hour crowd consisted of Black doctors, lawyers, judges, educators, government officials, politicians, professionals *and* con men, playas, low key pimps and drug dealers. The late night crowd was mostly street people— flashy pimps, dope men, playas, and wannabees.

When we first started shooting out the lights, our friend Mugsy would come through Lancie's to pick us up and we'd still go hit the neighborhood bars and after-hour joints. But we got so deep into drugs we didn't want to come out of the room for air. Not only did we not wanna come out of the room, we didn't want to come out of the bathroom—the dope fiend's haven. I loved it cause once the dope got flowing through my system, I would sit on the edge of the tub or on the toilet and just nod with the needle still in my arm. Whenever my high came down enough, I could jack the needle back and pump it once more. That worked as an extra boost, almost like shooting a fresh shot without adding any new dope to the syringe. Eyes droopy, head hung down or to the back.

And Mugsy saw it. He came to pick us up for the last time. We hadn't eaten or come out of our room all night. He saw the writing that we couldn't see. Disgusted, he shook his head "Y'all fool ass negroes gone kill y'all self" and he cut us loose. *Damn, I tried to think, Our boy done cut us loose.* I felt bad, but not bad enough to straighten up. "Pass that cooker," I muttered to Snap in a screwed up voice. More drugs was always the right answer. It wasn't long before I too called off work one time too many and the temp agency fired me. Our one-time weekend pastime became an everyday be all, end all. We basically began living in Lancie's. Snap hustled T's & B's, shot dice, and played numbers, and I started back working the streets.

I started working on the off-brand strolls. Most of the girls on these strolls didn't dress like thoroughbreds. They wore regular clothes. I later found out that one reason that some of the girls said they didn't dress up was because they didn't want their customers mistaking them for drag queens. The queens always dressed to kill. Of course, the queens had their regular tricks that were looking for them, but a lot of tricks couldn't tell the difference between queens and "fish"—queen talk for biological woman. Ever so often a queen or a trick would get sliced up because more than one penis came into play. I preferred to work between 69th and 77th and Euclid. That area along 55th near King's Bar and the Crawford stroll, that I worked when I was with Andrew, were considered low class, off-brand strolls because junkie hoes, renegade hoes, and drag queens worked them and only one or two value-added White girls.

Prospect from 40th to 22nd, Euclid from 55th to 30th were more highly ranked because mostly White girls worked them, they were downtown, and more White tricks spent money down there. The Cedar stroll that I worked when I was with AC was ranked somewhere in between. In pimp-ho circles the word was out that I had gone from a thoroughbred to a dope head. I didn't care what people said. I couldn't work on the other strolls because too many pimps patrolled them and Snap wasn't a pimp. A street girl is like a sheep among *hongry* wolves. Her life is under constant threat of gettin killed, cut up, beat up, robbed, raped and betrayed on the regula. Snap hung around a lot at first, but he eventually began to ease up on watching my back. He had his own hustles to attend to. This stroll was a little less fast-paced than others I'd ever worked, but still busy enough that I had to be alert and on the move.

The grouping was queens, fish, and O'Lady Shirley. Poor O'Lady Shirley. Word was that Shirley useta be a baad-ass thoroughbred ho, but you couldn't tell from looking at her that she was once an attractive money-maker. She had to be up in her sixties. If she wasn't, she sure looked like it. She was clearly worn out, with no figure to speak of. The deeply engraved lines accented by her pock marked dark brown face, held stories of death, abuse, and alienation, that even thick layers of liquid make-up could not hide. Her wig resembled an old dust mop. Though her lipstick was always fire engine red, she didn't have the speed needed to get first dibbs on a car. Even when she did get close to a car, most tricks burnt rubber on her.

In all my time working that stroll, I never saw O'Lady Shirley catch a trick. She had become an old beggar. As a last resort, she would stand near the transit house and ask the girls and their tricks if they could spare a few dollars. A lot of people wouldn't give her nothing. I did. She had worked the streets so long, she just didn't know what else to do with herself even after she couldn't make any more money. Sometimes when my mind was clear, I'd look at O'Lady Shirley as a wake up call. I wondered what in the hell I was doing with my life and I would ask God to help me. I was most reflective and religious on slow nights. A slow night is more dangerous than any other, because there are just less people on the streets and more opportunities for somebody to hurt you. My prayer:

"Lord if you let me catch one more trick, I'm gone for the night. I promise."

I got cool with a couple of girls in the area: Annie Mae and Freda Payne. Annie Mae was a shorter version of Tina Turner, except her nose was more African and her eyes were further apart. She wore a big ole smile, a big curly Afro wig, and big earrings. She had one of the best figures a woman could have. I mean, the sista was built-sturdy, toned and athletic-looking, with a neat waist and a nicely shaped backside. As nice as her figure was, she never wore revealing clothes—it was always long sleeves, thigh length long blouses with a thick belt over leggings. She had that strong country girl flavor. Freda was a thicky thick dark-skinned sister. Round face, big sexy brown eyes. I don't think I ever saw her smile. Laugh, yes; but smile, never. She wore her own neatly-cut short permed hair most of the time and she always wore black—a black dress, or a black blouse, with black slacks. Neither Annie nor Freda wore heels. They worked as a team most of the time. Not only did they watch out for each other, they were nosey as hell and they were always watching me.

"What's up, Ponytail? I see you out here. Yo man be down at King's selling pills. You can work wit us, if you want to. I respects a bitch dat gets money. This my girl, Freda. I'm Annie Mae."

"Nah, y'all the thoroughbreds. I be seeing y'all working ya thing. How the tricks ridin tonite?"

"It's always money to be made and tricks to be played!" Annie said as she slapped five with me as we began to stroll down Euclid.

We became get-high buddies. They introduced me to a whole nother level of the game and the wildest tricks in the world: Shitty Deal, Period Man, Feet Man, Undercover Fagg, Golden Showers. These guys rode the Cedar stroll but none of those girls would turn a trick with 'em. Word was that they were nasty and disgusting. But Annie Mae and Freda would take their money. Their philosophy was the weirder the trick, the more money. They told me more than I ever wanted to know about stuff that people do to get off. I mean, damn, if you need to do all that, what's the point? Annie and Freda could have won academy awards for how they acted with those guys to get them to empty their wallets and to keep 'em cumin back. Those chicks would have money when no one else would.

One thing about being a junkie is you gotta have get-high spots. I still had shame in my game and I didn't like going to shooting galleries and strange spots where I might be seen by people who knew me. When I didn't have any money and my high was supplied by Annie or Freda, I had to go where they wanted to go. They mostly went to a shooting gallery in the Outhwaite projects. For 5 bucks you got a new set of works (needle) and you could use the bathroom. I hated going there with them. Annie Mae had been shooting drugs a long time and she couldn't find a vein that worked. Her feet, her legs, her arms, and her neck were all dried up.

Once T's & B's and cocaine got inside my system, I felt like moving. Me and Freda would be ready to roll back out on the stroll to make money, but we'd have to wait on Annie.

"Freda, you and Ponytail got y'all medication in y'all, see if you can hit me, baby."

Freda whispers to me, "O, Lord, here we go, this dead ho cain't git no hit, now she gon' stop us from rollin." Annie got so frustrated when she couldn't get a hit. She would be sweatin and pokin and stickin and whinin. Blood would be everywhere. The bathroom would be hot as hell, and she would take off her blouse and try to get a hit in the only thing she had left—her groin. God! Not only are we in a bathroom the size of a closet, but she would start pullin down her panties, asking Freda to help her get a hit. Yuck!

Annie was so jealous of me because I hit a bulls-eye in my arm on the first try damn near every time I shot, and I'd be ready to roll out. My veins were fresh and healthy. I got tired of going through this scenario over and over and over, so a lot of times I tried to avoid getting high with them. I think, subconsciously, I began to avoid them too because I hated seeing Annie's body. Looking at her was like looking at my future—what 10 years of shooting dope does to a woman's body. Her body was war-torn. That's why she never wore revealing clothes. She had keloids, scabs, and abscesses from needle marks all over her feet, legs, thighs, arms and neck. In my mind, I'd be thinking, *It's time to quit when you get that bad.*

Like I said, my favorite get-high spot was the Lancie, but when I didn't want Snap to know how much money I was making and spending, I'd go to my friend Melvin's. I met Melvin through an old classmate, Lil Mike. Lil Mike was a stick up boy and every now and then, I would lure tricks down a dark off-brand street for him, and he would rob 'em and split the cash with me. I first started getting high over Melvin's with Lil Mike. It wasn't long before I started going through there by myself. Melvin loved me and I loved him. He loved me because I was a money machine, I got high all night and day, and every time I came through, I brought him a nice shot. He got high for free. His crib was perfect for me, because I had privacy. Although I sometimes felt somebody else was in the house, as far as I knew, only Melvin and I were there. His house wasn't a shooting gallery, so there was no in and out traffic. When I first began getting high there, he would let me use the bathroom and tell me to leave his shot in the cooker (a wine cap). After he got to know me better, we would sit at his kitchen table and get high together.

I do recall Lil Mike saying that Melvin was gay, but no one seemed to know for sure. But the more I got high at Melvin's the more I found out. One day Melvin was drunk when I arrived and he was talking like a queen.

"Mother Melvin is feelin alright tonight sugah. Can you spare a shot for my friend?" A neighborhood guy walks out of Melvin's bedroom and gets high at the table with us. Before long, they start making eyes at each other.

"Pony, you can let yourself out whenever you git ready," Melvin said as he and his friend went into his bedroom and closed the door. Melvin got to the point where he didn't care that I knew about him. I wasn't that surprised that he was gay. The surprising thing was the array of neighborhood men that he dealt with—husbands, boyfriends, and brothers of folk that I knew, and nobody else knew they were gay. I mean when you're a junkie hoe, people open up to you in new ways. Melvin and I became great friends. He was my Auntie. I could always show up at his house—anytime—and he welcomed me, no matter what or who he was doing.

Now I had been running around with Snap for about a year, and he was starting to get on my nerves. Number one, he was bad luck. Before we got together, I used to win gobs of money shooting dice with the fellas in the numbah house. I used to make my points so much that all the high rollers loved me. But once Snap started going with me, my luck turned. The high rollers stopped betting on me. I couldn't win for losin. Same thing with numbers. Before Snap started putting my numbers in, I used to hit all the time. But now, my luck got so bad, I couldn't catch two people talkin 'bout me. I started to feel like Snap was bringing me down. All he wanted to do was get high. He hit his little licks here and there, but he wasn't about progress. If I wanted to shoot my life away, that was alright with him because that's what he was doing with his life. I felt like that of the guys that I had been with, Snap was the worst because he didn't want anything. Now Andrew and AC might have been overbearing and abusive, but at least they had ambition. In a weird kind of way, I felt that I was better off with guys like them because two junkies together equals zero! There was one straw that broke the camel's back with our relationship.

This hustler asked Snap to front him a package and to hold his watch as collateral until he turned over the money. In the meantime, Snap went on a mission (a drug binge), got broke, and sold the playa's watch for some get-high. Snap started ducking this guy and that pissed me off because he could have got me killed. The first thing the guy did was come and find me on the stroll.

"Tell yo punk-ass man, if he don't have my watch by the end of the night, somebody gon' pay."

I was scared to death, but I tried not to show it. I knew then, it was over for me and Snap. I lost respect for him. Although I didn't want to be with a pimp, I was used to being with men who wouldn't duck and dodge nobody. That's one thing about Andrew or AC, they wouldn't take nothing from nobody. But now, I'm with a guy that is hunted. When this word got out, I knew I was a target for robbery, beat-downs and attacks like a renegade. I had to go back home to my parents' house, but I still sneaked around 69th and Euclid or 83rd and Cedar. On my work runs, I kept seeing this shiny new Black El Dog Caddy ride through. One day, I caught a glimpse of the driver. This fine dark chocolate brother rolls his window down, and rolls up beside me nice and slow.

"Lil Lady how you doin? You workin?"

I don't say a word, because I know he ain't no trick.

"Baby, you can talk to me. I been watchin you. I like your flava. You need to come get wit a real nigga, girl. Come on and ride wit me. I ain't no rapist or no murderer, baby. I just need a good workin girl in my life. Let's ride and get to know each other. You comin?"

I liked the sound of his voice, but I held my tongue and continued working my block.

The next time he came through, he parked his car, got out and leaned up against it. He was standing there in all his glory, finer than wine and 9 X 9. This beautiful man, looking as good or better than Billy Dee or Denzel. Smooth dark chocolate skin. Sparkly pearly white teeth. Soft-looking fro shaped and cut close to his well-made face. Trim waist. Just the right amount of hair on his strong chest and arms. Thick luscious well-trimmed mustache. If he had been in the right circumstances he could have been a model easily. But he wasn't a model. He was a pimp. He smiled at me, and I smiled back. A definite signal that I was open.

"What's your name, baby?"

"Ponytail."

"Oh, God is good, you talkin and smilin today!" he said, as he flashed them pretty whites.

"What's *your* name?"

"Mack."

"That's original," I said as I thought to myself, *Why you name yoself after a movie?* But I didn't care if his name was Puddintang, I knew right then and there, I was gonna be with him.

"Hey, I'm waiting on one of my customers to come through. If you want me to ride witchu, come back in a hour."

"I'll be back to scoop you."

I don't know what happened, somehow our signals got crossed and I didn't see him again for a few nights. In the meantime, I ran a background check on him trying to find out as much as I could about him. He definitely had street credibility, most of it because of an older brother who was known from coast to coast as an award-winning boxer. His brother could have gone pro if he hadn't caught a murder beef. Mack's father was known on the dope set. And Mack himself was known as an all around bad boy. He had served time in the fed joint for bank robbery. He "loved" working girls. Mack, his brother and their father were known throughout the Cleveland streetlife community. That was a proper resumé. I couldn't wait to see him again.

The next time I saw him, he pulled over, and apologized for not getting back to me sooner. I didn't ask what happened and he didn't offer. He popped the locks and asked if I was ready to roll wit him. I walked over, jumped in and slammed the caddy door. It was the beginning of a long and eventful ride.

When we first met, I immediately told Mack all about Snap. That I really wasn't feeling Snap anymore, and I wanted to be with somebody qualified and bonafide.

"Yeah, I useta be AC's bottom woman. Did you know AC?"

"I heard of dat clown-ass nigga. He was a damn good boxer like my brother, but niggas out here ain't on no boxin. You gotta bus a cap in a nigga's ass out here. Dat's how yo boy got took out. I heard he was a good playa though. Dat nigga knew how to bank dollas. I respect him for dat. You come from a thoroughbred nigga."

"Yeah, but I been on vacation wit dis nigga Snap. All he wanna do is get high all da time. He don't really want nothin outta life and I was starting to lose my goals. I always wanted to be somebody, to have something. Don't nobody wanna just be out here selling pussy to survive. I been thinking. If I'ma be out here killing myself, I need something to show for it."

"Baby, you makin the right choice hookin up wit me. I got other workin girls. It won't just be you out dere, that's too much pressure. Cain't no one Black girl, I don't care how thorough, get the kind of money necessary to make the type of moves I'm tryin to make—where we all can live good. I been talking to some Jew boys in New Yawk that gon' set me up in the diamond bidness. We gone have our own jewelry store. That's what ahm about. You worked in New Yawk befo?"

"Yeah, AC and Boe Leg took me up dere."

"Well, dat's where ahm headed."

"That's cool. You gotta talk to Snap though."

"I ain't gotta talk to dat lame-ass nigga. Word uh get out dat you wit me and I dare dat punk-ass nigga to say anythang to you. But let me tell you this. I don't fuck wit dope and I don't fuck wit dope fiend bitches. You fuck wit dope?"

"I have, but it ain't like I gotta have it or nuthin."

"Good," he said as he grabbed my arm and inspected it. "Cause I cain't have no junkie-ass hoe."

Now mind you, I had the beginnings of some track marks on my arms, but they weren't that bad yet. I know that Mack knew that I shot dope. Hell, everybody and they mama knew I shot dope. But I was still at a point where I could stop and I did. And it went down just like Mack said. I started back working on the class A strolls again.

Although I was "his woman" I was not emotionally attached to him at first. It was strickly business for me. At this point in my life, I wanted to get rich quick. I felt I had embarrassed my family and that if I could somehow legitimize myself, the fact that I started out as a two-bit hoe wouldn't matter. I needed to be attached to a powerful man so that I could be free to work the streets without harassment and generate the type of money I needed to retire. I liked the idea that Mack was connected with these New York diamond Jews. Our plan, as laid out by Mack was to make a few hundred thousand dollars, open a jewelry shop in Cleveland, and retire from the streetlife and begin our version of the American dream. This all made perfectly good sense to my warped 19 year-old mind.

When I first linked up with Mack, his stable consisted of his bottom woman, Nay, and me. Nay mostly worked on Prospect. Since I had long achieved my credentials among the Cedar girls and I knew that area very well, I returned to work there. At first, everything was cool between Nay and me because I didn't have any vested interest in knocking her from her throne. She had a daughter from a previous relationship, and I would sometimes braid her daughter's hair and babysit for her. One night Mack tells me that Nay is gonna work on Cedar wit me. Okay, no problem.

He said we should work together and look out for each other. Okay, no problem. Mack drops us off on the block.

"You roll wit dese bitches out here?" Nay asked.

"Whatchu mean roll wit em? We watch each other's back."

"Well, if you gone talk to dem broads don't talk to me."

"What in the fuck is you talkin bout, Nay. You cain't regulate who I talk to," I said with a torn up face.

"Ain't none uh dese broads out here no good. They on't like me and I don't like dem, so if me and you spose to be wife-in-laws don't fuck wit em."

I proceeded to talk to my girls on the block. They said they didn't like her because she thought she was better than other girls. You know the drill: she was light-skinned, had long flowing hair and she was slim in the waist and cute in the face. She was useta havin her way from everybody, including Mack. And, of course, she caught more tricks than dark brown-skinned girls. She wasn't a bad person, but when you got a certain profile, you have to carry yourself a certain way. Stuff just didn't add up in her favor. She didn't have that balance that is so important to streetlife. People gotta like you enough to tell you when something's bout to go down and at the same time, they gotta fear you enough to know that if they try you, it's gon' be trouble.

Later on that night when Mack came back to check our traps, Nay told him what was up between us. Mack gives me the science on it. Come to find out, he tried to work Nay on Cedar before I came into their picture, but she didn't like it because she had beef with some out of town chick. The chick sliced her face. Nay felt like nobody had her back, so she hated everybody that worked up there. Mack terrorized the block trying to find the out-of-town playa and his woman, but they got away untouched. Quite a few hoes wanted to warm that ass because Nay talked crazy to them when that incident jumped off. But they didn't touch her because "they peoples" was cool with Mack.

Nay always held Mack responsible for her face getting sliced and he kinda babied her because of it. I told Mack, I wasn't gonna stop talkin to people just because she didn't like them. I would look out for her, but she wasn't gonna control me. He was cool with it and told me not to pay that any mind.

Nay started working Cedar more often from that night on. I didn't mind at first, but she eventually started acting funny towards me. I think she wanted Mack all to herself, which I understood. He was gorgeous, plus she was with him before me. But Mack started playing both ends against the middle. Ain't no telling what he told her to keep her, but he started telling me that she wasn't qualified to be his bottom woman and that eventually, it was gonna be me and him against the world because we were kindred spirits. He started filling my head up to the point where I allowed myself to believe his hype.

I started getting busted continually again. Yep, Mama found out I was back on Cedar and restarted the Call the Police on Elaine campaign, so we hit the road for New Yawk.

•9•
Fools and Babies

WE THOUGHT OF OURSELVES as a dream team. Mack just had that look. Beautiful. Ain't no other way to say it. Panties got wet when he walked in a room. He had it all. He looked good in everything he wore and even better naked. The scent of his cologne, his nicely sculptured muscles, smooth cocoa brown skin. I mean a young girl got weak, or a weak girl weaker with eye contact. When we fell through an after-hour spot, heads turned. And, to be honest, Nay was beautiful, too. She was slender, fit, and naturally sexy. A Taraji Henson type face, with high cheek bones, like a real American Indian, thin but luscious-looking lips and piercing eyes. The sister knew how to dress, too.

I had it goin on too. Inviting, light brown, clear and sober white eyes. My innocent babyface with a hint of Tyra forehead. My breasts and nipples always at attention. And my biggest asset—yeah, you guessed it—powerful. To top it all off, I wore a superstar long wavy hair weave—the $500 bucks a pop type, that gave me that island look. Players would be all over me and Nay. When we walked in a New York after hour spot, we worked it like a runway. You had to show it, throw it and act like you know it. We got our propers. All kinds of alcohol and cocaine would be sent our way, but we'd turn it down. Mack would take the occasional drink and a joint. Nothing big. We were strickly bidness. Well, except when we came in for the evening. Mack would want to do it all the damn time.

He couldn't stay out of my room. All we did was "it." That was his way of making sure I was his and it worked—for a while. He was starting to want it too much though. Sex is just like drugs—You cain't git high on yo own supply *and* make money. That might be one reason I never really got that much out of sex. I wasn't trying to. I was used to faking it. I had to play a mind game with myself so I wouldn't feel like a total slut. I did like having sex with Mack though. I was in love with his good looks and the idea of being with a boss playa. That's all I could have loved about him. He had a rotten personality once I really got to know him, especially after he got strung out on freebasing.

We went to work every day late afternoon so that we would be on post to catch the after work traffic. Although my customers were pedestrians on 8th Avenue, the game was the same. Nay worked somewhere near 5th Avenue. We worked every night until 10:00 or 11:00 pm on the weekdays and later on weekends, depending on how dollars were running. The good thing about New York was that everyday new people were coming in town for vacations, conferences, etc, so we made as much money on weekdays there as we made on weekends in Cleveland, and we didn't have to work as long. But Mack was as bad as AC—a straight slave driver. We never ate a meal until the end of the night—maybe a bag of chips, a pop, or a candy bar. That was it. "Lazy hoes eat. Thoroughbreds clock dollahs." At the end of each night, we'd go back to our hotel and count up all the money, eat and sleep. Mack had a safe deposit box that he kept our money in. He wired money home to his family, bought himself jewelry, clothes. Nay bought all kinds of stuff for her daughter, her mama, herself and sent it back home. I didn't. I knew I couldn't send anything to my Mama's house. Mama wasn't having it. If I didn't earn money from a legit job, Mama wouldn't accept it—no money, no clothes, appliances, jewelry…nuthin! As far as Mama was concerned, I was gon' faart like a ackee muddah-in-law. (African American translation: I was goin out da worl ass backwards). So, I knew better than to try to send anything that way. I just bought clothes, kept my hair fly and put my faith in Mack, that we would buy enough diamonds to start our own jewelry store. After I got legit, then I could buy things for Mama that she never had the "oppachunity" to have. Dumb ain't even the word. We went on like this for months, until Nay had to go home. Something was up with her babysitting arrangement for her daughter. Mack sent her back to Cleveland by plane.

Mack started workin me really hard after Nay went home, and he was still wanting me to sex him all the time too. I started to pray that he would get some other women. After a couple of months, he finally caught a couple other chicks, a White girl and a dope lady. I was relieved in more ways than one. Things were going okay. I went several weeks without getting busted and Mack and I started getting close. One of the best nights of my life with him happened around this time. I remember vividly. I came in from work. And he was there waiting for me. I gave him a wad of cash, got out of my gear and went into the bathroom to shower. When I came out, he was sitting there in front of the mirror, staring strangely at himself and listening to Michael Jackson's "Lady In My Life" on the quiet storm.

And maybe through the years
Even when we're old and gray
I will love you more each day
'Cause you will always be the lady in my life

He led me over to him, sat me on his lap, and sang to me along with Michael Jackson. His off-key voice touched my heart and I knew that he loved me. It was wrong. How could a pimp love a girl that he was pimpin? "Playas only love you when they're playin." But at that moment I felt a deep bond between us.

"I dreamed about this."

"You did?" I asked.

"Yeah, when I was in the penitentiary, I dreamed of bein with a beautiful woman, who loved me and believed in me. It's you. You a good girl, Laine. I'ma take care uh you."

My heart smiled. It was like we were on a date that night, a date like normal people go on dates. He was sharing his dreams with me and they filled my brain. I didn't share my dreams with him. My dreams were pushed down in the corner of my foot.

"You smart. That's good. That's gon' help us with the jewelry bidness. These other broads I got up here, they don't mean nuthin to me like you. You come befoe dem. Cause you got in on the ground flo. KnowhatImean?"

"What about Nay?" I asked.

"What about her? Ain't nobody here now, but me and you, you knocking all dese broads out da box. When the dust clear the air, it's gone be me and you standin there. You love me?"

"I do."

"That's all dat matters."

I should have asked him if he loved me. That's what really mattered.

I was bringing home some serious bacon. The White girl was too, and we were loading up the safe deposit box. Word got out that we were "hittin em good." Folks from Cleveland followed us lock step and landed in the promise land. We ran into quite a few of 'em: "Skillah and his circus"—that's what people called 'em—Candy's dude with the White transvestite and crew. Pimpin Rob, the brother with the tallest hooker in Cleveland; Kenny C; and this one playa that only had one White girl, Pimpin White girl V. I mean, it was like somebody yelled "It's gold in dem dere hills." Mack didn't want nobody to know where I worked. He didn't want none of his friends' women working near me on 8th Avenue. It was a cool spot. Not that many people worked the area and I was able to make White girl money on the regular.

A pimp is chosen by other women based on how "good" he treats the women he already has. I was polished. I looked, dressed and lived like a "bout it" street girl. Little did I know, Mack had been tryin to "knock" another hooker that worked my block. She was serious, always busy, darting in and out of taxis and the transit hotel. She was tall, very attractive, cocoa brown, statuesque, curvy, large but well-toned with a Venus Williams shaped backside. She wore her hair permed with a long wet and wavy piece on the back. She carried herself like a true pro. The moment she opened her mouth to me, I knew I would like her:

"I watch how you flex and hangle yuhself. How you focus pon dollahs. Move like you serious and try reach someweh." Immediately I knew she was Jamaican and that made me like her even more.

"Yuh mon, Mack, tol me that you guys are from HOhio."

"Yeah, you from here by way of JA?" I asked.

"How you knuo so good?"

"My family is Jamaican so I must know Jamaicans."

"Mack always aks me to jine your famalie, but I doan like how he move."

"Why you say that?"

"You doan knuo? Well, if you doan knuo, I won't tell you."

From that day on, we always spoke to each other. She called me Miss Ohio and I called her Miss Jamaica. It bothered me that I didn't know what she was talking about. But deep inside, I didn't wanna know. I did notice how Mack left me unchecked a lot. I just thought it was because he had the White girl and the dope lady. With Nay outta the picture, it was just him and me against the world. Yeah, he had other women but he didn't love them, just like I didn't love none of the tricks I had sex with. We were both strickly bidness. I was very loyal to him. I figured maybe Jamaica saw Mack with the White girl or something and she thought I'd be jealous.

One balmy New York night, as I was soliciting on the corner of my block, Jamaica caught a nice big fat tourist. I don't know where he was from, but it wasn't America. Jamaica was a native New Yorker, so she could smell a tourist a mile away, especially one that had a fat ass wallet. She approaches me arm in arm with this huge WWF wrestler lookin dude:

"Yow, H'Ohio, come nuh mek wi parti wit dis sweet mon and meki enjoy imself. He can pay us a 5 undred dollah—come wid us!" she said angelically.

I knew the drill from working with Candy what was about to go down—at least I thought I knew. When we got into the room, we went into our routine.

"Ooh, ahh" moanin and groanin as soon as we walked into the room. We started unbuttoning his shirt, pants—caressing and undressing him.

"Baby, we gon' give it to you like you never had it befoe, all night."

My job was to keep him from watching Jamaica. We had him on his back with his pants around his ankles. I pulled up my skirt and straddled his face, while Jamaica got the rest of his money out of his wallet. Everything was working perfectly until he started getting suspicious. He started trying to push me off of his face before she could get the wallet back in the pocket. I struggled to keep his face in the place but he overthrew me. I jumped up and out of the way, as he began searching wildly through his pants for the wallet. As he jumped to his feet, Jamaica threw the empty wallet to him and flicked out a long blade:

"Muddafucka if you mek one wraang move, I'll cut out ya bloodclot eart," Jamaica declared in a voice that I didn't know could come out of her mouth, as we both began backing out of the room. "Our mon right outta door in dis allway and ya betta don't come outta dis bloodclaat room until we gone or your ead gonna get blow off, ya 'ear?"

"Please, Please, Please, don't do this," WWF begged.

We backed out of the room and ran for our lives down the stairs, out the transit hotel and for the nearest taxi. That's one thing I loved about Manhattan, the taxi service! It was like boom.

We hailed a taxi and got dropped off a few blocks over. Jamaica paid the driver. We hopped out and went into a nearby restaurant. There, we counted out and divided our booty. Adrenaline pumped, as we laughed in whispered breaths, replaying for each other how the sting went down. We both had well over two grand each and we decided we'd earned the rest of the night off.

"Promise me you nah give yuh mon none of dis money."

"Why you say that?" I replied in a high shrill. "He's my man and we tryin to do somethin with our money. That's what we came here fuh."

"HOhio," Jamaica sighed as she looked at me like I was the biggest trick in the world. "Mi ago show you someting. You mus come wid me. It ah di only wey. You mus see. Come!"

She led me out to the street and flagged a taxi. I don't remember exactly where we went, but we ended up in what reminded me of Vincent's place in Cleveland, except I didn't see a bar. It was sooo crowded and smoky. Jamaica held my hand and guided me through a smoky maze of people—provocatively dressed women and mostly sharply dressed men—until we got within eye and earshot of what Jamaica wanted me to see... Mack, sitting there with a pipe in his mouth, surrounded by smoked out hoes. They were all up on him, rubbing on his private parts, working him to buy them another piece of rock. I mean, he was sitting up there trickin, smokin with these hoes—smokin up my hard earned money that he was supposed to be stacking for our jewelry store. I grabbed Jamaica and held onto her for dear life.

"How could he do this? He a dope fiend? An undercover base-head? Oh, God. Help me God. What am I doin? I hate myself. I hate him. I hate everything!" I began to cry uncontrollably.

"Is alright. Is alright," Jamaica said as she patted my back and hugged me. "Hey, You still ago gi im ya money?" She asked as she gently shook me and looked into my eyes.

My voice was gone. I couldn't talk. What little spirit I had evaporated from my body into thin air. I was broken. "Take me outta here," I quivered. As we left Smokers Paradise, Jamaica tried to offer me a sense of direction and hope.

"You doan haffi be wid no mon, ya knuo. I doan have no mon. I wuk fuh my owna self. I knuo New Yawk. You an me can help one anedduh. He doan neva haffi knuo weh you mek ya lass trac. Come. We can stick togeddah an put wi owna money togeddah an big up wi self."

"Jamaica, I can't think right now. I just wanna go to my hotel," I cried. If I hadda had the sense I was born with, I would have taken Jamaica up on her offer because my life took a turn for the worse after that night.

I took a cab all the way back to my hotel room, in North Bergen, New Jersey, to clear my head, to think of how to handle things. I ran myself a hot bath. I scrubbed and douched as though I could clean the filth of my life up with soap, water and vinegar. I sat there in the tub, crying, thinking about how he had sang his heart out to me, how it was him and me against the world:

You will always be the lady in my life. . . .

I thought back to all the times he sweet-talked me, tellin me how he had dreamed of being with a girl like me when he was locked up in the penitentiary, how much he loved hookers, that I was his girl, and how successful we would be. When I added it all up, Mack came up short. And, I came up even shorter. I was the biggest trick in the world. I had turned hundreds, if not, thousands of tricks, big, small, tall—I fucked the rainbow, risked my life, used my body like a machine. Went to jail. I was stupid enough to believe that all my suffering and loyalty would be rewarded. I thought the jewelry store would give me self-esteem.

The dope lady Mack had turned out to be the real playa. She got him strung out, and then dumped him. She was in business to make money, not support somebody's habit. He couldn't terrorize her either because she was backed by some New Yawk brothers that would have had his ass for breakfast. He didn't earn half as much money as I did, not even with his White girl, because he couldn't keep her long enough. The White girl found out about him before I did and bounced.

I thought to myself, *He wanna be a drug addict. I'll show you how to be a drug addict, nigga, I'll shoot the lights out. I know how to shoot my money up befoe I'll let a nigga smoke it up.* I planned to slow way down on my trickin, stack me some dollas, return to Cleveland, and shoot me some dope. That was the plan.

I had peeped game on the 8th Avenue stroll. I could tell who the junkies were. I slid up to this one chick one night and asked her if she could cop me a bag of cocaine and some works if I paid her. Bingo. It was on. We got a taxi. She directed the cabbie to the cop spot. She came back out and gave me mine. She asked me if I needed a place to do it. "Yes, I do," I said in righteous determination.

"Cool, I don't usually take people to my apartment cause I have a kid. But I been seeing you. I didn't even know you got high. I thought you was strickly bidness."

"I was. You know who my dude is right?"

"Yeah."

"This is between me and you. It ain't his business what I'm doin."

"I gotchu."

And with that, she led the way to her apartment, which was actually in the same building as the transit hotel on the corner of 8th and 38th. Her old man was there. He got high too but not like she did. They had a kid together and he was her babysitter, so he only dibbled and dabbled. They both couldn't be strung to the max. This would be my first time doing a whole bag of USNY drugs by myself.

It was stronger than anything I had ever had in my life! Totally off the chain. Usually when I shot dope, if it wasn't that potent, I could run the whole syringe in and then wait about 10 minutes and jack the rest; but this dope was so strong, I couldn't even run the whole syringe. I had to wait. I sat there in her kitchen waiting for the bells to stop ringing in my ears. I was frozen. My host finished cooking up her rocks and began smoking her stuff. I was just sitting there damn near comatose when the lady of the house stuck her pipe in my mouth and told me to take a draw and hold it. I helplessly obeyed. I sat there with a needle in my arm and a pipe in my mouth. Only the Holy Ghost himself kept my heart from bustin open wide. I was right up there with the stars and the moon.

"Brenda!" Her old man, yelled. "You gone kill huh. Don't do that!" I could hear him talking but I couldn't open my eyes and I couldn't talk. I was damn near dead. My lips twisted, my teeth grinded, my fingers moved—as though each had its own brain.

All I could do was sit there and wait for the bells to subside. Thank God, I hadn't fallen into the trap of the world's most scandalous druggies. My hosts were actually nice. They could have helped me OD and then robbed me—I had a wad of cash under my wig, and she knew it because she was out there working too. By God's grace, her old man snatched the needle out of my arm and made me drink some ice cold water. Slowly but surely I worked my way off of cloud nine. Brenda's old man made me eat something. I could only take a few bites. Cocaine kills an appetite. Slowly but surely my mobility came back and was able to get a taxi back to my hotel.

I promised myself I wasn't gonna get high no more in New York. It was just too risky. Two dope fiends together equals disaster. I knew that from being with Snap. But every moment, the thought just kept rolling through my mind: *A junkie bitch ain't shit. . .I don't fuck wit dope fien hoes.* I couldn't believe that Mr. Bidness had fallen prey to cocaine. It started to show, too. He lost a lot of weight. He was starting to pawn his personal jewelry so I knew the safe box was empty. Although I hated him for what he did, I felt like if I left him up there alone and he died, I wouldn't be able to live with myself. After all we had gone through, I cared about him in some kinda weird ass way. At this point, even though I had gone through a junkie hoe phase, I still had control over my addiction. Or so I thought, since I could go for long periods of time without getting high. I thought if I didn't get high and I kept the clear head, Mack would be able to see what he was doing, how he was throwing away our dreams and that he'd snap out of it. He knew that I knew that he was hooked and I wasn't in any hurry to be giving him money to blow up in smoke.

He became a maniac, houndin me to make more money. He'd come to our hotel in the wee hours of the morning to get the money that I'd made that night. If the sum wasn't hefty enough, he'd go off: "Bitch, this all the muthafuckin cash you made? Let me see your arms. You been shooting dope?"

"Naw, I ain't been shooting no dope, Mack. I paid up our rent for the month. We can't be up in this city living from day to day."

"Bitch, did I tell you to pay up the rent? I run this hoe. You don't run nuthin but yo muthafuckin mouf."

"Why I got to be bitches and hoes all the time? If I'm such a bitch and a hoe, I must be a good one. You ain't starvin'. If you is starvin', its cause you out here fuckin up our money."

"It's cause you a sorry ass hoe. Shut the fuck up." *Whop!*

He'd start beating me. I would scream so that the hotel manager or anyone could hear and come to help me. When he would come home in a rage like that, the only thing that would calm him down was sex. To keep him from hurting me, I'd have sex with him to make him fall asleep and leave me alone. Can you imagine? I didn't even enjoy sex. I was a sex dealer. My motto was: "Hurry up and c__ cause I'm not havin fun."

I see all these prostitutes on talk shows claiming that they love sex and they love selling it. They have something that I didn't, because I had to brainwash myself with tricks *and* with my man when I was in bidness. When I was with my man I had a psychological block and I couldn't enjoy it because deep down inside I felt if I got into it he would believe that the real me was really a whore. When I was with tricks I had to act like it was the best thing since sliced bread because that made them spend more money. The whole thing was insane.

A few incidents happened that made Mack finally decide to come back to Cleveland. One day we were walking down the street in Manhattan and Mack and a White cop made eye contact. Now it was obvious that Mack didn't have the sense he was born with, because he barked at a cop: "What the fuck you lookin at?" Before I knew anything 3 or 4 cops swooped down on him and they all seemed to disappear into the crowded street, but just as I began to panic, I was able to follow his screams into the alley of a precinct. They dragged, taunted, poked, kicked and prodded him with flashlights and billy clubs. I ran behind them screaming, yelling, and begging, "Please don't kill him. He's all I got. We came here together. We not from here. I don't have nobody else, please!" They made him beg before they let him go:

"I'm sorry, I'm sorry off-i-cers," Mack cried slowly in between shallow breaths, "I won't do...I won't do it again."

I was grateful they let him go because even though I did walk the streets by myself many a night, the street people knew I had a man and they'd think twice about doing anything to me. If word got around that he was in jail or if people didn't see me with anybody, it would be open house on my butt...well you know what I mean.

Another out-of-the-blue flukey-type thing happened. One day Mack and I were walking down the street on 8th Avenue and this crazy dude started talking to me, saying what he wanted to do with me and that he would kick Mack's ass. At first, we just kept walkin and tried to ignore him. But the more we ignored him, the closer he came toward us.

"Man, go on about your business. You not gone do nuthin to nobody."

Mack picked up a stick and the guy charged him. I spied a thick green quart-sized glass ginger ale bottle lying on the ground. I picked it up and sneaked up behind the guy and wacked him across the back of his head with all of my might. It was just like I had patted him on the back.

He shook that off and said "Oh, I'ma have to kill yo bitch, now." Wildman started coming towards me, and Mack whopped him in the back to detract him from me. By this time, a beat cop saw what was going on and ran over to assist us. The cop caught hell with this guy. They were madd tussling. It was like this guy was on steroids and speed mixed together. It seemed like he had the strength of at least three NFL players. Luckily, two other beat cops ran over to support their comrade in law. They handcuffed Wildman and off they went. Mack and I were like, "What in the hell was that?"

And if that didn't take the cake, my near death incident in the transit hotel made me lose all hope. I went into a room with a trick, sober, alert and on my job. I did everything systematically, just like I had always done. Everything was working perfectly. The customer was done in five minutes or less. I popped up and continued to get myself together so I could go back out on the stroll. As I was going to open up the door for us to leave out of the room, the trick grabbed me by the back of my neck and started choking me. I couldn't scream and I couldn't breathe. I mean it was like the stuff you see on TV and think it's phony. But it wasn't. He knew where to hold his hand on the gland in my neck to cut off air to my brain. I woke up, I don't know how many minutes later. I was partially clothed, I had been raped and my purse was gone.

Now what was I gonna do? I couldn't call the police because hoes can't be raped. From the perspective of the law, I am wrong. All I could do was try to get myself together and leave the room. When I got outside Mack was out there. He said he at first thought that something might have gone wrong but he pushed it out of his mind hoping that I might have come up on some other date already inside of the building since that happened all the time, but that wasn't the case. The trick had only gotten back the money that he gave me which was in my purse. I never kept any accumulated cash in it, only condoms, make up and fake ID. Mack took me to the clinic and I was tested for VD. A few days later, I found out I had been infected with an STD and I had to lay up, take my meds, and nurse myself back to health. I was more than ready to go home to Cleveland.

During this same timeframe, Mack got a call from home. His sister was sick. She nearly died in childbirth. That was the only time I ever saw Mack cry. And with that, we left the big apple to return to The Mistake on the Lake.

When we got back, I was mostly depressed and hopeless. It seemed that my life was just one bad episode after another. Of course, I was still workin the streets and I got an apartment in East Cleveland. I was dibbling and dabbling as far as shooting drugs. Mack didn't keep a heavy watch over me because he was spending most of his time at Nay's house. Sometimes I would sneak back out on the stroll when he would think I was in for the night. One night I sneaked out on 77th and Euclid to make some fast cash. Rushing like that caused me to go against one of the cardinal rules of street walking: Never get in a car wit a young Black dude. I jumped in this guy's car and told him to pull over. As soon as I jumped in, he grabbed me. As I struggled for the door, he hit me in the back really hard. My back was killing me. I felt this dull throbbing pain. He told me to keep my head down or he'd kill me. I said, "Hey, you want some free pussy. It ain't worth killing for. Just please wear a condom. I'll *give* it to you." He pulled over on some dark street far away from where he picked me up. When we got there, he led me out of the car and instructed me to lie down on this back porch. I was hurting too bad to resist. I just begged him not to kill me and to please wear a condom. He did neither. This was one of my many deaths. My back was burning so bad,

I just wanted him to get off of me. After he finished, he told me not to try to look at his car when he pulled off. I assured him that I wouldn't. When I was sure he was gone, I got myself together as best I could and crawled out to the main street. It hurt every time I tried to stand up straight, but I finally managed to stand up. I could only take shallow breaths. I walked for what seemed like a country mile before I came upon an all night convenience store.

"Pleez call…an ambulance…for me."

"Hey, she bleedin. Hey ma'am you been shot?"

"No." I panted. "I think…I been…stabbed."

I looked down and I could see that I was standing in a puddle of blood. The ambulance came and took me to Mt. Sinai Hospital near Wade Park. Not only was I stabbed, my lung was punctured. The doctors asked who did it to me. I told them what happened. The best thing they could do for me was tell me to stay off the streets. I called Mack and told him where I was. He sent Nay to come and see me. Ain't that a bitch? He sent Nay instead of coming himself. She also returned the next day to drive me home upon my release. Mack had the nerve to be angry at me because I shouldn't have been out that night. I was burning mad at his ass too.

I was getting tired of a lot of things. Mack was spending a whole bunch of time at Nay's. When he wasn't at Nay's he was bringing strange women to my apartment trying to get them to be with him, while I would be out working. That infuriated me. I came up with a bright idea. I thought (the same dumb ass thought that so many young girls think) *I done invested too much in him. If I get pregnant by him, he'll straighten up, get out of the game and*

make a family with me. Not long after I decided to get pregnant, I did. I hid it from Mack as long as I could because I knew he was not going to be happy.

When he found out, sure enough, he was mad as hell. "You think that baby mine, but you don't know fa sho. Why on't you get a abortion? It ain't none of mines."

"Nope, I'm havin it. I know it's yours."

I thought I had his ass just where I wanted him. I thought having that baby was gonna give me some type of say so in our lives together. Huh! The beat went right on. He still expected me to work and I did, up until my late months. Come to find out, Nay was also pregnant by him. She was six months ahead of me. He was sitting up babying her, letting her work whenever she wanted to.

My addiction at this point was still "controlled." When I found out I was pregnant I stopped getting high. When I started showing too much, Mack moved me into his mother's house. His mother was pretty cool with me, even though she thought that I was corrupting her son. Anyway, I made sure I paid her for living in her home, and I bought groceries, even though Mack said we didn't have to pay her.

One day I took my big belly to the clinic for an appointment. Nay had already had her son by Mack. I don't know why she was there. But there she was—alone. I was sitting in the waiting area. She came and stood over me. She started loud-talking me, calling me all kinds of bitches and hoes, telling me that I should have an abortion because I was having a trick baby.

"Talk to ya man. Stay outta my face. I'm sittin here mindin my own business," I said in the New York dawg that I had acquired, as I contemplated how I was gonna get this broad up off of me. Where I'm from, when people start running off at the mouth, something has to go down. I watched her out of the corner of my eye, waiting for the opportune moment, when her mouth was open and she felt really confident that I wasn't gonna fight her. Yoke! I grabbed her around the neck and headlocked her with all my might. I turned my body to the side because I knew she was gonna try to kick me in my 9 month belly. That's the kind of chick she was. The clinic security guards and an old neighborhood friend saw the commotion and ran over and broke it up. They wrestled her down to the floor and contained her, because they saw that I was pregnant and that she started the altercation. They escorted her out of the clinic. A few days later, I went into labor.

I was home alone, over Mack's mom's. I called the ambulance for myself. When I got to the hospital, I called and called and called Mack's mom's house. No answer. It's like they knew I was gonna have my baby and they didn't want to be there with me to find out what the baby was. Ain't no thang, I can take care of myself. Neither Mack nor anyone from his family came to see me while I was there. They all liked Nay better than me. I called the only person who was always there for me…Mama. Even though I broke her heart a thousand times, Mama came to support me. I only briefly thought of how much this woman loved me. I was too deeply lost in my own world to appreciate her at the time. But Mama came to the hospital. She held, hugged and kissed her granddaughter. Mama loved us unconditionally. I named my baby girl after Mama, Evelyn Richardson, hoping that would show Mama that I wanted to do better. Mama and her friends bought gifts for the baby and took me back to Mack's mother's house when I got out of the hospital.

Only spending one night there, Mack quickly moved me to an empty apartment that belonged to one of his sisters in the projects down the way. Because I was always reaching out to his family and begging for their friendship, when they came around to "visit," I knew they were only coming to see if my baby looked like him. I thought to myself, *I don't care what it look like, it's still his, since he claimed all the other fruit of my womb!* No one could deny that my daughter looked exactly like him. He couldn't care less. He hardly ever visited us. He was just waiting until I was well enough to go back to work. I wanted to go back to work too, because I was mega depressed and I needed to ease the pain of my life. The way I saw it then was the only good thing that happened to me was my beautiful baby girl. She was so cute and she loved me. She didn't care that I was a prostitute or a loser. All she knew was me. Even though I loved my daughter, it wasn't enough to deter me from hitting the stroll in less than six weeks. I paid one of Mack's sisters to babysit for me, so I could get back to what I had come to know best.

•10•
Death Cycle

EVER SINCE I WAS a little girl, bits of self-love had been creeping out of me daily. Mama and Daddy's big fight. Every time I got the message that "regla" Black girls weren't beautiful. Every time somebody looked at me like they wanted to fuck me. My first date/ rape. When I killed my baby. Every boyfriend that couldn't see me. Every trick I turned. Every betrayal of my loyalty. Every shot of dope. Every beat down. Every dollar I gave Mack or any man. No matter how "down" I was for him, he couldn't love me enough.

And how could he? He was just as soul sick as I was. My intimate experiences with men up to this point in my life were all unhealthy. None of them ever saw my beauty. And even when they got a glimpse of my heart, it still wasn't enough. There was a commandment that got left out of the Bible: "Thou shalt not love a girl from the hood." Yes, my family loved me, yes my parents were hard working people, yes they took me to church and taught me right from wrong. But that was never enough for any man of mine, and it wasn't enough for me. Instead of believing in who I was, I allowed myself to be defined by people, places and things. I was caught in a struggle between what the rest of the world told me about myself, and the girl my family tried to raise. When people did or said things that hurt me, the only way I knew to fight back was to get high. It was my way of saying "Fuck you!"

By now, I was "livin" between my parents' house and my apartment in East Cleveland, and jail (either the Cleveland House of Correction or the Justice "just us" Center). Most of the times Mack came to our apartment was when he was on one of his smokin binges or to date another woman that he was trying to pull in. When he was sober, he stayed with Nay and their son. He never took other women to Nay's crib and he never let Nay see him at his worse. He always saved his worse for me. He loved their son more than he loved our daughter, and I hated myself more for that, too. Sometimes I could feel when he was gonna come to our apartment in a rage, and I would take the baby and run disappearing to my parents' house before he came on the scene. I applied for welfare and was getting a check, food stamps and medical. The check wasn't enough to cover the rent and utilities for my apartment so I always kept in touch with a few of my regular tricks so I could pay my bills. Plus, my "regulars" supported my habit without me having to work the streets. At first, I could get my mom to babysit, go turn my regulars, shoot a bag of cocaine or T&B's and come back home in a couple hours. Eventually, one bag wasn't enough. After a while, a couple hours started turning into a couple days. Whenever I came home, Mama would fuss:

"Hey girl, you a mother. You suppose to be at home wid your chile. You love dis baby? If you nuh wan dis baby, let us go downtown and you sign over dis baby to me, cause you goin on like you don't want har."

"Yeah, I want my baby Ma." I'd always say. I'd go take a bath and sleep and regroup for a couple days. I'd wake up to my little daughter sometimes in the bed with me. I'd look at her and feel happy and promise myself, my baby, and God that this was my last time.

But somehow, I couldn't keep my promise. Mama knew what I was doing, and some people would say that she was co-dependent, or enabling me in my addiction, but she didn't want to banish me from the house in fear that I'd be somewhere dead or mistreated and she'd never know what happened to me. She just prayed that I would wake up one day, before I got killed or O.D.'d. So she never said she wouldn't babysit but she wanted me to do better. I would do okay for a week or two. Then my addiction would take over and I would tell myself "I ought to be able to just shoot one bag a dope and come home like a decent human being." I couldn't see that a "decent human being" wouldn't want to shoot drugs.

Mack and I got into this weird pattern. Every time I worked the streets, I was a fugitive on his most wanted list. He would comb Cleveland's streets hunting for me. Sometimes he'd be sober and sometimes he'd be "fienin." All of our encounters were now abusive. One time he rode down on me on a night that was raining moneymen for everybody—queens and fish. I was working on 63rd and Euclid. A warm gentle mist of rain sprayed the streets with a clean rain smell.

Tricks were riding, back to back and I was catchin left and right, just like back in the New York 11th Avenue days. Before I knew it, I had a fat wad of cash. I decided I had enough money to get off the street, cop, go over Melvin's and shoot the lights out. I stepped into the bar on the corner of 64th to catch my last customer and a ride. Just as we walked out the door, there he was:

"Hey, where you goin?" He asked with that, "Bitch I gotcha" look.

"I got some bidness to take care of. I'll meet you back here in a few, okay?" I lied.

"Nah, come on ride wit me."

"Mack, I'm bout to take care of some bidness, what's wrong witchu?" I pleaded as I shrugged behind my customer.

Mack bogarded him, grabbed me by the arm and started shoving me towards his car while my customer ran and jumped in his car and sped off.

"Bitch, you think I'm a goddamn fool. Get yo ass in da car."

"Nah, Mack, I'm not goin nowhere witchu. You done ran my trick off. I ain't goin nowhere withchu!" I shouted to the top of my lungs, hoping someone would come out of the bar or jump out of a car or off of a light post to save me from him. But no one came. I knew what was next. So I curled into a ball up against the building that housed the bar. He began punching me. First, in the stomach, then in the ribs. I begged him to stop, and I kept my face covered, because I never wanted to be a toothless hooker, and I didn't want my face disfigured.

"You gone give it to me, or do I have to beat it outta you?" He growled, as he stopped punching me momentarily. "Bitch you wrong. You got my baby and you ain't no mutha. You ain't nevah home. You be leaving dat baby over yo momma house and you out here selling pussy to buy dope. You a dope-fien-bitch and ain't nobody gone help you."

"You don't give a fuck about our baby. All you care about is Nay's baby. Fuck you!"

And that's the last thing I remember saying before I saw lightening and fell to the wet ground near the curb in front of the bar. He must have kicked me everywhere except my face. He got my wad of cash, as I lay on the ground in the fetal position. I remember hearing his car door slam and the sound of burning rubber on the road.

I lay there on the ground thoughtless and sobbing for a few minutes. Killed again. I pulled myself up slowly and looked around. With every move I made, I felt invisible kicks all over my body. Miss Pam spotted me and ran over to me:

"Miss Thinnng," she sighed in her affected drag queen falsetto. What happennned? Who did dis to youuuuu? You want a ambulance, gurrrrl?"

"No," I panted in a shallow breath. "I just...need to go... somewhere...where I can take a bath...and shoot some dope. Can you lend me some money?"

"I just got out here, Miss Thing, but yo girl Freda Payne up the block. Come on bay, take yo time. I'll walk you up there."

I crept up the street holding the hand of Miss Pam for what seemed like an hour. With every step, my ribs, my arms, my back, my legs, my butt ached. Miss Pam yelled for Freda, who ran up to meet us as we got closer to 69th and Euclid, one of Freda's favorite corners.

"Aww, Pony, yo nigga did this to you? You need to press charges on his ass befoe he kill you. Fuck dat nigga, girl. Fuck him!"

"Freda... I cain't go home like dis," I muttered.

She took one look at me and signaled over to her waiting driver to pick us up. She instructed him to take us to Lancie's. She took me to her room, ran a hot bath for me and went to fetch us some food and drugs. She took care of me, helped me get some decent clothes and let me lay low.

After a couple days, I turned up at my parents' house, with a fractured rib and a battered body, and so the cycle went... .

I was the type of drug addict that could go quite a few days without getting high; but after a while, the urge would be so strong that I couldn't control it and I would take my chances, hoping that I could outsmart Mack. Plus, my addiction got to the point where I needed a fifth of Wild Irish Rose and a couple bags of dope in my system to feel anything.

I started being paranoid all the time, and I would take chances I wouldn't normally take. On more than one night, I was nearly murdered because I was always in a rush and I didn't use my better judgment. One thing about hookin, misreading a face could mean death.

One night I was working as fast as I could between 55th and 63rd on Euclid. I had made a little money but I wanted to catch one more trick before leaving the block. As usual, I prayed, "God if you let me catch one more, I swear, I'm gone." Soon as I prayed that prayer, a dude rolls up in a dark van, the door swings open. I didn't look good before I leaped. As soon as the door shut, I got a bad vibe. I looked at the door, no interior panel and no handle. I looked in the guy's face and saw death on it. He looked like a black Grizzly Adams. A big bushy head of hair and a bushy beard. He had alligator shaped teeth that protruded in a way that wouldn't allow his mouth to close. I looked in his eyes and all that was there was death. I turned to him while he was driving and cocked my left eye to the back of the van to see if we had company. I knew about how guys would hide their friends in the back of a van and pick up unsuspecting girls and train rape 'em. I couldn't see anything back there with my one eye. It was dark as hell and I could tell no seats were back there. But I did see what looked like a shot gun barrel on the floor between the arm rest and the driver's seat. My mind started flashing on how I was gonna get away. I tried not to panic as I began talking shit:

"Baby, we gon' party tonight! You ain't got to spend no money. You drink?"

"Yeah, you got somethin?"

"Don't worry about nuthin. We gone git some wine, we gone get a room and we gone fuck all night. How bout dat?"

"That sound good," He stated slowly in a low wicked grumpy bass voice.

I had already turned to him, unbuckled his belt, unzipped his pants and started rubbing his genitals while I was talking to him.

"Baby, you married? My pussy so good, it'll make you leave your wife."

"I know yo pussy good and my dick is too."

"I know it is. Hey, pull over. You see that store, pull over right here. I'm gone run in here and get us some wine and we gone do it up all night. Open the door." He pulled over just like I asked. All the time, I could hear and feel my heart beating fast and hard inside my chest. But I knew I couldn't let him know that I was terrified. I'm steady praying in my mind, "God if he open this door, I swear, you ain't nevah gotta worry bout me no mo'. Lord, please let him let me outta here." I prayed that sincere prayer to the Almighty God and he heard me. Grizzly Adams reached between his door and his seat (Lord, I liketa peed on myself) and pulled out what looked like a long hanger wire with a hooked end. He reached across me and skillfully stuck the wire into the door and unlocked it. I pushed the door open, looked at him and grinned, "Wait right here, baby. I'll be right back" as I jumped down and out the van.

I went in that A-Rabb store, reached under my wig, pulled out my cash and snatched a twenty off my little roll (all without breaking my stride) and handed it to the A-Rabb at the cash register:

"Please let me out the back door, somebody outside and they gon' kill me if I walk out dat front door. Please let me out the back." I thank God to this day that that A-Rabb told one of his boys to lead me to the back and let me out.

Now, I had to get out the streets in a hurry. I couldn't go across Euclid to head toward my parents' house. That was too risky. The only way to avoid Grizzly was to stay in backyards as much as I could. The back of the A-Rabb store faced Chester Avenue. I ran as fast as I could and darted across Chester, staying in backyards, ducking in doorways, and generally trying to be invisible, until I got to Hough Avenue. One of my junkie friends, Bit, a little skinny older woman I met through Freda and Annie Mae, lived on 82nd and Hough. By God's grace, I made it to her house with no sign of Grizzly. I needed a shot of dope and some wine when I got there.

I rapped hard and fast on Bit's door. It took her forever to look through that peephole. But when she did, she was glad to see me, cause she knew I either had some dope or was about to buy some. And lucky for me, there was a pill man and a couple of other people in Bit's house that night sitting around shooting the lights out. As I copped a fix from the pill man and sat down to get high with Bit, I told her the whole story of how this dude was gone try to kill me and how I tricked him into letting me out of that trap van. We sat around for hours, like dope fiends do, talking, shooting dope and drinking. A few hours later, the 11:00 o'clock news came on and who did I see: Grizzly hand-cuffed.

I don't know how I was sober enough to pay attention to the TV, but I noticed it and screamed in high soprano, "Biiittt!

That's da nigga I was telling y'all about. Dat's him right dere. Das him! I told y'all. I knew he was gon' kill me. I just knew it." Come to find out, he was a serial killer. He was connected to the murders of more than 20 prostitutes between Ohio and New Jersey. When they flashed his face across the screen, everybody agreed that he looked like a killer. I had to be off my game to jump in his van. That was the topic of my conversation for a long time. God allowed me to escape death—once more—this time from a serial killer rapist. You would think I would have kept my promise to God then, but I couldn't.

Mack had terrorized most of my get-high spots. He was getting so bad on my trail that some dope men stopped selling to me or they'd call him when they saw me. The only places I had left to get high were Melvin's and One Eye Ted's. Melvin had some mean pit bulls. When someone knocked on his door, their barking would make you think the end of the world was at hand.

Despite the security of Melvin's, it got to the point that I couldn't get high in peace there. Mack had found out and he'd come over and bang on Melvin's door. I'd be so nervous and paranoid that I'd run and hide in one of Melvin's closets every time I got high—whether Mack came and banged on the door or not. One time I ran into one of Melvin's closets and jumped in a bucket of mop water. I was so paranoid, Melvin had to talk me out of that closet like the police talk a suicidal maniac off of a ledge. Melvin soon grew tired of Mack coming over his house, and I didn't want to keep putting him up to lying for me, so I started making my visits over there few and far between, as best I could. I needed a new spot.

I knew One Eye Ted from back in the day when I was a little girl around the neighborhood. His son was one of my brother's friends. Ted left Cleveland many years before, but had recently returned. He was a friendly older dude, a hustler who had a White girl that everybody called White Girl Brenda. I ran into him in the neighborhood grocery store one day and come to find out, he and his girl lived around the corner from my parents' house, on 72nd and Carnegie, close to Lancie's and the Euclid stroll. *And*, Ted loved to get high. Bam! There it was! A new get-high spot for me. White Girl Brenda didn't shoot dope but she loved to drink and snort cocaine. She worked on 77th between Carnegie and Euclid. We devised a little plan.

One Eye Ted would sit in his car on the Euclid end of 77th and White Girl Brenda would stand on the Carnegie end. They both kept an eye for Mack for me. If they saw a car or a shadow that looked like him somebody would whistle and I would dart back behind a building or a car. I was able to work like that with them for a good little while. And I was comfortable getting high at their crib. Until one day, I went over Ted's and I noticed that his front door had been kicked in. I wondered what was up. Ted said I should leave and not come back again. He told me he was gon' have to shoot Mack if he ever came back to his house and he didn't want me to be caught over there. I felt bad about Ted's door. I offered to pay but Ted just wanted me to leave. Mack got the word that they were harboring me, that I was working with them and hanging out over there, and he searched their house like he had a warrant. He basically ransacked the people's house.

Not only did Mack go over Ted's, he also started going over my parents' house looking for me. He told my mother that I was a drug addict and that he was trying to help me clean up my life, so I could raise our child right. He took the cake with that one! By this time, I had let our apartment in East Cleveland go. I never moved my stuff out or went back. I just abandoned it. Mack knew I was staying at my parents' house and he never came there to see our daughter, but he got to the point where he was so strung out that he was starting to go to any lengths to track me down. He didn't fool my mother though. She didn't trust him and she knew I was terrified of him.

Mama was at her rope's end with me. She kept asking me to sign over my baby to her and sometimes when she was really flabbergasted she'd ask me how come I didn't just drop dead. It hurt, but I couldn't stop myself. I was pretty thin and my dope fiend episodes were getting worse and worse. If I wasn't out getting high for two weeks straight, I was in the City Jail or the Cleveland House of Correction, the Work House. More than once I caught a 30-day sentence at the Work House. Though one part of me hated being locked up, another part of me was glad. Jail made me rest and have 30 days straight sober. One time when I was getting out of jail, I noticed a flyer in the "just us" center lobby. It was about a program that helped prostitutes and sexually exploited women. It was called Project Second Chance and it was based at my old school, Cleveland State University. Somewhere deep inside of me I wanted to go back to school but I didn't know how. I contacted Dr. Edwards who was the head of the program and I began to meet with him. He was a nice small built brown-skinned Black gentleman. He spoke very kindly and gently. I remember how deeply concerned he seemed to be with helping me get my life on track.

I told Dr. Edwards everything. I told him how I was on drugs, a prostitute and my pimp was my child's father and I felt trapped. I told him that I knew about AA and that I had gone to meetings but I wasn't an alcoholic. I knew that drugs, pimps and prostitution were killing me. He asked me lots of questions about myself and my history with men. And I remember feeling like if I worked on things that we talked about, I might be able to get it together, but pretty soon, I would start missing appointments. The main thing that messed me up was I would always get high again and that would throw me off track.

Same thing with AA. When I was in a meeting, I would hear what seemed to be logical principles of AA that could work for any addiction, but as soon as I got a strong urge, I could twist those principles to my purposes. They told me if I could just not take the first drink or drug, that I'd be alright. But I always told myself I wasn't an alcoholic so what they said didn't apply to me. I needed to know how to stop shooting dope. I felt if they could teach me that, I'd be alright. I just kept hoping that one day, I'd be able to do one bag of dope, have a drink and go home, like a decent human being! Getting high and turning tricks, turning tricks and getting high. I couldn't do one without the other.

Since we'd lost our apartment, Mack started renting a room in the Town House Motel, not far from where we used to live. The Town House didn't draw as many of Cleveland's streetlife people as Lancie's, but it got its fair share. Sometimes when Mack would catch me, he'd take me there with him. Our relationship was far past infatuation. I didn't like him as a person. He didn't like or know me. To him, I was just a dumb ass junkie hooker that had a kid by him. Sometimes I felt sorry for both of us and I would just stay with him because there was nowhere else to go. I would work for him for a few days and when I couldn't take it anymore, I'd run away.

• 173 •

If I was leaving our daughter at my parents' house to be with him, it was alright; otherwise, I was the lowest bitch on earth. One time when he caught me, he kept insisting that we get high together. He thought that I would stop running away and that we would somehow get closer if we bonded in drugs. Now out of all the years that he and I had known each other, we never ever got high together. Mack was always violent when he had drugs in his system. I knew it wasn't going to work. But what could I do? What I said carried no weight with him. Mack was used to smoking cocaine—freebasing. Back then, they didn't call it smoking crack. He breaks out with a big bag of cocaine and two brand new sets of works and asks me to hit him.[1]

"Mack, I ain't gon' stick no needle in yo arm. You gotta do that for yoself," I said as I fixed up the medication and drew us up two syringes full. I tied up his arm for him watched his virgin veins rise and handed him his syringe.

"Come on and hit me."

"Nah, you ain't gon' be able to blame that on me. Do your own dirty work," I said as I got a hit and began running my dope in my arm. In less than a few seconds I felt a strong surge of heat go to my brain and through my system. I snatched the syringe outta my arm and walked out of the bathroom as my heart pounded a hundred miles a second. In this elevated state of mind, I began dusting the room.

"Come in here and help me."

"I'll be there in a minute, did you get it?" I asked as I began cleaning off the dresser.

"Biiyiitch.. what the FUCK you doin? Git in here and help me!" Mack screeched in a scary voice that even I had never heard before.

---

1   *Inject drugs into him.*

I opened the bathroom door. Blood—on the floor, streaks on the walls, on the shower curtains, and running down his arm. Mack's eyes bulged and his breathing was out of control. "Look what you did bitch." I grabbed a towel, wet it with cold water and patted across his forehead. He snatched the needle out of his arm and was still and quiet for a moment like he was listening to a voice on a different frequency.

Suddenly he grabbed me by the throat,

"What you be doing with all dem niggas you be gittin high wit?"

"All what niggas I be gittin high wit? What you talkin about?"

"That fagg, Melvin, that One Eyeded nigga, them ho's you be with, Bitch. You thank I'm a damn fool. Yall be fuckin," he said while tightening his grip on my throat.

"Mack, you trippin, baby, you trippin. Let me go," I barely cried out.

At that point, he started ramming my head into the porcelain bathroom wall. As I screamed and begged him to stop, I almost gave up, wishing I was dead to stop the pain. The thought popped into my foggy mind that he wouldn't kill me if he remembered we had a child together.

"Mack, this is me, Elaine, we have a daughter together. You trippin, stop, please stop. You gon' kill me."

He eased up off me. He was sweating and looking real crazy.

"You just need to rest. You not used to shootin up. Here, take off your clothes and let me bathe you, so you can calm down," I said as calmly as I could, not bothering to look after myself. I could feel that I looked like the elephant man. I just concentrated on getting him to relax, so I could make my escape before he decided to shoot up again and beat me. I took off his clothes and got him to lie down on the bed. He started fondling me. I eased away and went into the bathroom to tidy it up and run his bath water.

"Hurry up, I want some pussy."

"Okay, come on, baby, your bath water is ready. I'm gonna go get some ice to put on your head. I'll be right back. I love you," I said, as sweetly and softly as I could.

"Nah, bitch you ain't goin nowhere."

"Mack, stop actin so weird." I pleaded. "This is me, Elaine. Your child's mother. I love you. I told you not to shoot up. You not used to it and you trippin. I'ma get you some ice and give you a bath, you understand?"

"Yeah." He said. Just as I turned to head for the ice bucket and the door, he continued: "Wait a minute, Bitch. Take off yo muthafuckin clothes."

"I'ma take my clothes off when I come back. I'm getting some ice fa you and fa me. Yo brain is on fire and my head and face all fucked up and we need some ice, okay?"

"Like I said Bitch, if you try to walk out dat door wit ya clothes on, I'ma fuck you up. Strip and go git da ice, bitch."

"Ok," I said as my confidence evaporated, my voice quaked, and my insides shook, because I knew I was gon' have to make a run for it butt naked. I didn't have a choice.

I took off all of my clothes except my panties and my heels, got the ice bucket and walked out of the room. As soon as I could, I slipped out of my heels put down the ice bucket and blazed down the stairs and past the front desk. Heads were spinning and turning as I flew by. I didn't know where I was going or how far I would get, but I figured I'd take my chances with him killing me on the streets. I didn't feel like dying that night in that room. I ran as fast as I could and as far as I could down Euclid Avenue. Thank

God, it wasn't winter. Cars were pulling over, blowing, honking, people were looking and pointing. I would run a couple blocks, and then walk a little, all the time looking around, hoping that Mack wasn't after me. Finally, I made eye contact with a kind and gentle face. When this man pulled over for me, I jumped in his car and just broke down. I told him to get me away from here and not to stop until we got to a police station. He took off his jacket and gave it to me to cover myself, as we drove to the police station at 152nd and St. Clair Avenue.

The kind gentleman led me to the counter and told the police that he found me running naked in the middle of Euclid Avenue. I didn't want to make trouble for Mack. I could have told the police that he was keeping me in the hotel against my will, that he was there with drugs, but our whole story was too complicated. How do you explain to the police that you're a prostitute that just wants her freedom to work the streets and support her habit? How could I explain that he was my child's father and my pimp? No matter what I said, I would be a no good woman getting what I deserved. So, I just said that my boyfriend beat me and put me out of the hotel and that I needed to go to a battered women's shelter. The officer remarked, "Your boyfriend, huh?" as if he knew that there was a lot more to the story.

"Yes," I said very impatiently. "I need help. I need to go to a shelter." The nice man who brought me to the station was determined to wait with me until he was sure they found some place safe for me to go. After a little while, a woman officer brought me an old shirt to put on. I went in the bathroom, and without looking in the mirrors, I put on the shirt. I didn't want to see myself. When I came out, I gave the nice man his jacket and a hug. It seemed like it took forever for the police to make arrangements for me to stay at the shelter. But two male officers finally came to take me. One of the officers cracked, "Hey hon, hang on to your shirt. Let's go." They laughed and chatted as we made our way to the car and all along the way to the shelter. My mind kept flashing between Mack ramming my head in the wall, running down Euclid Avenue naked, and people laughing at me. "How did I get here?" Every now and then I would repeat in my mind "God will help me. God will help me. God will help me."

Before we reached the shelter, the officers pulled over and let me out of the car. As I exited, two women greeted me. They identified themselves as shelter workers and explained that they keep the location of the shelter secret to protect the clients. I was cool with that. I got into another car with them and pretty soon we were there. It was a big house somewhere on the west side. There were women, children, different kinds of people there. I just wanted a hot bath and a nice bed to sleep in. I don't remember much about the first night, except the people were kind, I was allowed to take a shower, to eat and I was given a comfortable bed to sleep in.

The next morning I met with a social worker, who asked for a lot of information: Did I have kids? If I was married? Did I drink? Do drugs? Stable place to live? If I exchanged sex for drugs? If I was on welfare? I told her about my daughter—that she was at my parents' house and that I knew Mack was gonna go there looking for me and I didn't want to go there for a while. I asked if they could get me an apartment. She asked me if I lived with Mack and I told her that we had lost our apartment and what my situation was, that he would force me to work for him or stay with him and that our relationship was abusive. Well, it was evident that I was abused from the knots on my head. To her question about me exchanging sex for drugs, I told her, "I make money. I'm not a strawberry." That's what we called women who exchanged sex for drugs. "I'm a professional. I can set up shop anywhere and make more money than suckahs who work a square job. I make my own money and buy my own high," I said indignantly.

In a sincere quiet voice, the social worker woman asked me, "Well, what would you like for us to do?" She knew my mind wasn't right and she spoke with compassion, because even though I was at the end of my rope, if she had spoken harshly to me, I would have left that shelter and told her to kiss where the sun don't shine!

"I need y'all to help me get an apartment, and get my daughter, so I can be safe," I said in a lowly voice, with tears streaming down my face.

"Miss Richardson, if you don't stop using drugs, getting an apartment won't do you any good, because you'll go back on the streets and you'll be vulnerable to be attacked by your perpetrator. The first thing we're going to do is to get you medical services. If you want us to help you, you will participate in our mandatory in-house meetings—AA, cycle of violence classes, and parenting classes. You can stay here for up to 90 days and we can start the process of finding you an apartment if you follow all of our rules."

I had been to AA meetings before, but I had never heard about the cycle of violence and I didn't think I needed parenting classes. *But, okay*, I thought, *I'll do anything y'all say. Just help me.* I stayed so high that I didn't remember that I had missed my period until she told me that I would be going to the doctor.

My medical exam revealed among other things that I was pregnant again. This time, I didn't know who the father was. Always on the run from Mack, I got so careless on my drug missions that a condom must have slipped off, or had a hole in it. As much as I douched my insides out, douching doesn't prevent pregnancy or disease. It's mostly cosmetic. Thank God, I didn't have gonorrhea, syphilis, or HIV. I had liver damage and a mild case of hepatitis. The doctor said it would go away if I stopped drinking and drugging.

Life in the shelter was all right. I did everything they told me to do. I washed dishes, swept, mopped, did my share of cutting up vegetables, or whatever I was asked to do. After a few weeks, the social worker arranged for my daughter to be brought to me.

Things were looking up a little and I really wanted to straighten out my life. In general, everybody in the shelter got along like family. There was one sweet old White lady, who was around 70 years old, in the shelter that everyone called Grandma. She really acted as if she was everyone's grandma, helping everybody with everything. In the violence meetings, Grandma always argued against the instructors when they taught us that we should *not* go back to our perpetrators, especially if that person is unwilling to go for help. Grandma said she had been with her husband 50 years and she was going back to her home and he wasn't gonna kill her and she wasn't afraid of him. She said that every meeting and in every interaction I had with Grandma, she always said it. Grandma did just what she said she was going to do. When her time was up at the shelter, she went back home to her house with her husband and sure enough a few weeks later, Grandma was dead. Her husband hit her in the head with a hammer and killed her. It was the lesson of the battered women's shelter that stayed with all of us more than all the meetings in the world. I made up my mind right then that I would never go back to Mack again, that I would never be with any abusive man. I knew I had to kick my habit or I was gonna die.

By the time my 90 days were up, the shelter got me into an apartment. I got a lot of donated household items from Catholic

Charities and moved to the far west side of Cleveland. I didn't know the neighborhood or anyone in it. The shelter social worker put me in touch with AA meetings that were close to my new neighborhood. I also started going back to Dr. Edwards' Project Second Chance appointments. I was doing well, keeping my prenatal appointments and going to meetings. I had it in my mind that I would never go back on the streets and I would stay sober one day at a time. Every now and then, I'd get the urge to get high, but I fought it by praying and remembering that if I just didn't take the first drink or drug, I wouldn't have to worry about my life becoming unmanageable.

It had been months since Mack had gone to my parents' house looking for me, so I felt comfortable going back there to visit. I would stay a few weeks at a time. I made it all the way to my ninth month and the urge hit me. One day when I was at my parents' house, the new me agreed with the old me, that I could do one bag, have one drink and no one would know. I called Melvin and asked him if he could cop for me. He was very happy to help me out. I didn't want to ask Mama to babysit because I didn't want her to know what I was up to. I took my daughter over my girl's house, an ex-hooker that I ran into at a clinic appointment. She had retired and was only doing business with her regulars. She had a couple kids and she had moved into the neighborhood. I told her that I just needed her to keep my daughter for a few hours, so I could get high. I wasn't planning on going on the street or anything, I was gonna sell my food stamps, and hang out over my boy Melvin's and get high. She was cool with it.

A few hours turned into the next morning and all my foodstamps were gone and now I was in full fiend mode. My next source of cash was to call my old faithful customers. I had one in particular that never let me down. I could ask him for anything and he'd give it to me, if he had it. He didn't even want any sex, he just felt sorry for me that I was pregnant and needed drugs. He made me swear that if he bought me a couple of bags that I would go home when it was all finished. He hung with me for a couple days, until I had run through four or five hundred dollars of his cash and then he cut me loose after he saw that I could never get enough. I mean I could go a whole week with small 2 to 3 hour breaks in between but steadily shooting drugs.

After I burned him out, I went through my list of regulars whose phone numbers I had memorized. One of my regulars was a Cleveland Police officer whose beat was my area. When he saw that I was pregnant, he helped me to scam quite a few potential customers. He would be in his patrol car and park in a hidden location. I would get in the car with a customer and get them to pull to a certain spot and to pull their pants down. Within seconds, my Policeman would pull up behind us with his flashing lights and siren, put a blinding light in my customer's face and tell me to step out of the car. The customer would be so happy that my Policeman let him go, he wouldn't dare complain that he had just paid me for nothing. My Policeman helped me like this for a couple of days but he soon saw that I was sick and needed to get off the street. The last time he helped me, he made me promise that I was gonna go to the hospital or home, but I didn't. When he stopped helping me, I continued to contact regulars.

Some of them gave me money without a sexual transaction because they felt sorry for me that I was a pregnant woman strung out, but I had to have sex with some of them too. Some even wanted vaginal intercourse, but I would talk them out of it. I was able to go for about another week just on the strength of regulars. But pretty soon, I had burned out all my cash flow. I had to go back on the streets. By now, I hadn't seen my daughter in about two weeks. The minute I hit the streets, I found out that the word was out that I was on a binge and that my brother wanted me to bring my baby home. I sent word that my daughter was at Fannie's house. In a few hours, word got back to me that my brother got my daughter from Fannie's and took her home to my mother. I looked a mess and I was a mess. A pregnant, tired, drugged out paranoid matted wig wearing hooker.

•11•
The Gift of Love

THE STAPLES OF MY DIET were cocaine, T's and B's, and plain Lay's Potato Chips. Now and then someone would suggest a chicken wing. To keep my blood flowing, I topped off these nutrients with a shorty of Wild Irish Rose, or a quart of Colt 45 malt liquor. My *regula regula* was running in and out of Melvin's house all hours of the day and night. In surprising moments of clarity, I would remember that my baby should have been born and I'd be truly sorry for what I was doing but I couldn't stop. My catnaps began to torture me. I saw Mama's face echoing Grandma's words, "Yuh nuh gi weh pickni, yuh gi weh puss and dahg. Grandma sacrificed Mama's "oppachunity" to get an education, so that maybe someone in our family down the line could get one. Why couldn't I, right here in the so-called land of opportunity, sacrifice for the baby in my belly and the one I dumped off on Mama? Grandma's and Mama's words haunted me; but I wasn't fit to raise any child. I couldn't even control my own mind.

Where was that girl who loved to learn, sing, play the violin, and who loved her family and friends? I was an addicted corpse carrying a fatherless baby into hell. There was only one way out—the hospital.

"Melvin, I need an ambulance."

"You in labor?"

"No, the baby is dead. I ain't felt it move in a long time. I need help to get it out. Can you call the ambulance for me?"

"Yeah baby, you gone be alright," Melvin said as he dialed Emergency Medical Services and put me on the phone:

"I'm way past nine months pregnant. My baby hasn't moved in a long time. I been shooting drugs for about a month straight. Can you take me to the hospital?"

I gave my name and location. In no time, the ambulance arrived at Melvin's and took me to Metro Hospital. I told every nurse, doctor, and medical attendant that looked at me that I had been shooting drugs for the past month straight and that my baby was dead. Puzzled eyes in shaking heads glared at me as if to say, "What is this world coming to?" I didn't know anything except that I needed to go to jail for what I had done to the baby.

After a thorough examination, the doctor confirmed that my baby was alive. Alive? I couldn't believe it. Alive? I didn't know if I should be happy or sad. The doctor said that I needed nutrients. They started me on an IV and told me to eat as much as I wanted. The hospital's food wasn't all the great, but I ate lots of graham crackers and pineapple juice. A few days went by before they decided to induce my labor.

At the appointed hour, she arrived. The nurse tried to hand her to me but I just waved her away. I was tired and afraid. I didn't know if she was Black, White, or what. All I knew was that I didn't want to hurt her anymore. The doctor told me that they were going to keep my baby under close observation and run some tests on her to see if there were any drugs in her system:

"Miss Richardson," said the doctor, "If your baby tests positive for drugs, we will have to report you to state authorities and it is very likely that your child will be taken from you and you will be prosecuted."

"Good," I said.

Jail would be a good place for me so that I wouldn't be able to get high or turn tricks or embarrass my family. I didn't know if my family would keep this baby too.

I laid in my room feeling sorry for myself. After a while, one of Dr. Edwards' graduate students from Project Second Chance came to visit me. I don't remember how anyone knew I was in the hospital. But this nice little young White woman came to visit me. She held my hand and talked to me.

"Hi Elaine, how are you feeling? You remember me from Second Chance, right?"

"Yeah, I remember you. I'm tired," I muttered.

"It's great that your delivery went well and your little baby girl is here."

"Yeah, it's great," I said without feeling.

"I'd love to see her. Would you like me to bring her in?"

"No," I said.

"Have you seen her yet? I know she's beautiful. Every child is a gift from God. They are so full of love. She knows you and loves you already.... You carried her all those months. I know you have lots of doubts and fears, but everything's gonna be alright. You are beautiful, Elaine. Yes, you are beautiful and you have lots of love to give her. You're not a bad person. You just made some bad choices. Everything's gonna be alright. You'll see. It's just gonna take time and work, one day at a time. I'm gonna go get your daughter."

I cried as I listened to the little young White lady's soothing sincere voice. I wanted to believe her that maybe there was a little hope for me. A few moments later she came back with a little red baby.

"Here she is, Elaine. She's beautiful," she said as she handed me a small and cozily wrapped up baby. I studied her face and right away I knew who her father was. He was a kind short thin light-brown skinned Black man, but I had forgotten his name and I didn't know how to contact him. She was a cute little red Black girl and I loved her—a nice little baby. All of her fingers were there. Both of her eyes. Her little lips and face. The perfect shape of her head. Her whole body. She was all there. I didn't know what was going to happen to her or to me. But I decided right then what I would name her—Ebony, because she was a pretty Black girl. In a shaky and humble voice I admitted to my visitor that I needed a new mind and I needed to start working on it right away. She cautioned me to take my time that I should work on one thing at a time. Her first suggestion to me was to begin attending the hospital's AA meetings. She promised that Project Second Chance would do all it could to support my recovery.

In the days that followed, I went to every AA meeting the hospital had. I listened carefully to every word anyone said about staying sober. Although I was still afraid to bond with my baby, I visited her often in the newborn intensive care unit where she was kept in an incubator because of her low birth weight and suspected drug addiction. I was afraid to call my family. And I heard nothing from Mack. My daily visitors were a social worker and the young White student from Dr. Edwards' Project Second Chance.

"D day" finally came—the day when I would find out about my baby's tests. A male doctor and one of the female nurses from the intensive care unit came to give me the results:

"Miss Richardson, you are free to take your baby home. It's a miracle. We don't know why, but she tested negative for drugs.

She is sound. You should be very grateful. Besides your six weeks check up and the feeding schedule we've outlined, your aftercare includes recommendations from our social work department that you continue to attend AA meetings, that you attend parenting classes and continue to work with your other support systems. We wish you all the best." Along with that news, the doctor gave me a nice firm handshake and a smile. I was in shock as the nurse wrapped her arms around me and gave me a big hug. I couldn't believe what I heard. They couldn't find a trace of anything anywhere in my baby. Yes, it was a miracle. God was giving me another chance. Before my new baby and I headed for my parents' house in the taxi that the social worker had arranged, I thanked everyone who helped us—all the nurses, aides, the social worker.

As we entered the house, my little daughter ran to the door,

"Mommee here, Mommee here, Mah mee here!" She sang and danced, anxious to hug me and see the baby. Mama had fixed up the downstairs let-out couch for Ebony and me. I was so lucky that my family hadn't thrown me away. They had all kept love in their hearts for me, and I was glad to be home. Afraid of myself, I rehearsed everything I heard at AA meetings over and over again in my head, especially the rule that I needed most, "Don't take the first one."

I hadn't been home a week before I called AA and they sent someone to take me to meetings. It wasn't long before I heard a young woman at an AA meeting tell a story that resonated with me. The story that this young woman told sounded so much like someone I knew from the block, but I figured it had to be a coincidence. The woman telling the story looked like the movie star, Lynn Whitfield—long flowing hair, clear light glowing skin, beautiful face and smile. The woman I knew looked like a hard core street dyke—matted hair sticking out from under a dingy scull cap, over a hardened frowned face. She continued to discuss incidents that happened to her while she sold drugs near 130th and Kinsman and down the way on East 55th Street. She talked of her addiction, how she went from sugar to shit. She talked of how alcoholism and drug abuse robbed her of years of her life, how so many people that she knew and loved had died of unnatural causes linked to drugs and alcohol, how she saved herself, became a mother to her son and turned her life around through working the program.

At the end of her talk, I went up to the front of the room to meet her and sure enough it was her—all beautiful and sober. I knew right then and there that she was going to be my sponsor. I thought, *If God can help her, I know He can help me!* We exchanged phone numbers. I couldn't wait to connect with her. She was a for real down to earth sister. When I called her, she took the time to talk to me. I told her all about things that had happened to me, how I shot dope from sun up to sun down, how I had worked the streets off and on in and out of town for over 6 years, and how I didn't know who one of my daughter's father's was. Even though she hadn't worked as a prostitute, she was a recovering drug addicted woman from the streets, so she knew where I was coming from.

Veronica was a great role model for me. She had been clean and sober three years when she became my sponsor. She was an extremist just like me—whatever she put her mind to, she went all the way with it. We went to meetings together religiously, all over Cleveland. Even though neither of us had a vehicle, getting a ride to meetings was no problem. Everyone in the program knew her and loved her because she was such an inspiration. She was a great mom to her son. He attended every meeting with her, so I felt comfortable taking my two girls along, too.

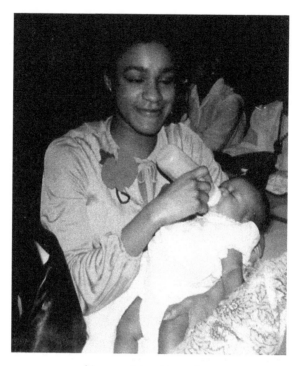

My second daughter and me

I needed to love and feel good about myself again, but feelings of shame attacked me all the time and threatened to stunt my growth. It's like qualities that we need to live are the same ones that can kill. Take boldness for example. I was a bold bitch, when I worked the streets. I would come out of the dope spot, right across the street from Sardis Baptist church, early on a Sunday morning, wearing my gear (really half-dressed) and looking the dignified good Christian folk dead in the eye as they marched up in the church. I dared one of them to look at me out of the corner of their eyes and even give me an inkling that disapproval crossed their mind. I would have read them from Genesis to Revelations about how so many of their brothers and husbands were my customers or were homosexuals.

I had to learn how to live all over again. Now I needed that same boldness to walk pass the dope spot with one baby in a stroller and one by my side up into Sardis. I looked straight ahead wondering what the dope men had to say about me but at the same time determined to get every little bit of inspiration I could get from church. I hoped that the church folks didn't know I was the same half-dressed bitch that used to spit at them. If you know anything about old school Black churches, you know that you have to be bold to walk up in there with babies out of wedlock. I once heard somebody say ain't nuthin worse than a reformed ho. And that was me. *Hongry*, I went to AA meetings, parenting classes, Project Second and church like my life depended on it.

Going to church and hearing the word of faith helped me. All the things that I had done wrong, I had to learn how to forgive myself. I had to learn how to forgive other people, too. Even though I knew this in my mind, I still couldn't erase all of the resentments out of my heart overnight. It's a process. Even now, some of the hurtful things that people said or did to me are still buried so deep down in my heart, that I don't even know they are still there until they creep up. It's a struggle. My desire to get well has to outweigh my hurt. So when things well up in my mind, I ask God to take these issues out of my heart so that I can get better.

My fear of wrecking my life began to lessen as I remained sober, one day at a time. But I still had nightmares. I would be sitting in a bathroom somewhere with a needle in my arm and I wouldn't be able to pull it out. And I would be screaming and crying. I would be afraid that I had let my daughters down, that my parents wouldn't be able to keep them for me anymore, and that I would lose my family. Veronica said it was normal to be fearful and that having a little bit of fear was good for me.

Although I was *hongry* and bold, I did care about what people said about me. Everybody in the hood knew that I had worked the streets and I didn't want people to say that my babies were trick babies. So, I made it my business to connect with Mack's family because I wanted them to acknowledge my kids. Afterall, they never denied that my oldest daughter was their relative and I felt like they owed it to my girls to treat them equally. I thought that since Mack had reaped all of the benefits of my womb, that he ought to claim and be responsible for whatever came out of it. I wanted Mack to be a father to my daughters—both of them.

But it wasn't long before I realized that I would have to stop stuffing my kids down their throats. Although Mack's family was never mean to my girls, they made a difference in how they treated them. And, Mack didn't bond with my daughters. I confided in Veronica about these fears. One thing that she told me that I had to do is to forgive Mack and his family. She said I had to realize that everybody is dealing with issues and that people have to deal with their own stuff before they can love other people. She said if I carried around in my heart that he or his family owed my children something that I would always feel hurt. I had to realize that it was hurts that were down in my heart that would lead me back to drugging, drinking, and working the streets if I didn't let them go. Homegirl had a way of saying stuff to me that just sunk in: "Girl, don't nobody owe nobody nothin. You get what your hand calls for."

Did my hand call for me to end up like O'Lady Shirley? Layin up with old men to pay my bills? Negative. Be on welfare for the rest of my life? I liked having money too much for that. Thank God my parents always had my back, but I needed and wanted to stand on my own two feet. I figured that school might be an option. I knew I wanted to go, but I didn't know how to go back.

For one thing, if I went back I would be 27 years old—an older student. Something about being an older student was scary to me. Did I have the brainpower that the 18 year-old freshmen have? Would I look stupid asking questions? I had been out in the streets. Would anybody recognize me? Who would babysit for me and how would I pay for it? What did I want to be and what should I study? How would I pay for everything? On one of our visits, I shared all these fears with Dr. Edwards and his associate, Paula. They assured me that where there is a will, there is always a way.

Dr. Edwards helped me get all the necessary paperwork filled out. Because I had been academically dismissed from Cleveland State University, I had to petition to be readmitted. I applied for every kind of financial aid and support program that I was eligible for. One program that helped me a lot was the childcare provider program. A really good thing about the program was you could ask someone you knew and trusted to take childcare classes and become a certified provider. And that person could keep your kids. I knew just the person I could ask—our next door neighbor, my play aunt. The kids called her Tauntie. She was a staunch Christian woman who prayed for me when I was strung out. Although she was a little nosy, she was a good person, who would do whatever she could to help me. It was a win-win for Tauntie, since she babysat for a couple people anyway. Becoming a certified childcare provider for the state guaranteed her pay. There was still one thing standing between me and school...the books. I had never returned some Art History books to the CSU library once I got kicked out of school. I had been out of school a long time and felt like the lone-ranger. I was convinced that CSU would investigate me and turn my petition for readmission down when they found out. Dr. Edwards assured me that all I had to do was return the books. But I was full of fear—I thought everyone in the world knew that I had worked the streets and that CSU would refuse my application. Dr. Edwards told me to bring him the books and that he would return them for me. And he did. Not long after, I found out that my petition was granted. I was accepted back into CSU.

With a six-month-old, a three-year-old, six months of sobriety, and all the support that I had behind me, I figured I would put my all into school or die trying. Afterall, I had run out of tricks.

•12•
The Cleveland State University Years

SCHOOL WAS AN EASIER grind than flaggin cars, duckin undercovers, jumpin out of movin vehicles, dodgin bullets, turnin tricks, outsmartin serial murderer rapists and killers, runnin away from pimps, and stayin high. Six months after I had my baby, I was back in school, desperate for a new identity. No more wigs, make-up, high heels, g-strings, and jail cells. I wanted nobody there to know me, or where I'd come from. I covered myself with my versions of proper English, square clothes, and square dealing. I was just glad that I was alive, with a new lease on life. My new outlook was working in Introduction to Sociology and Basic Algebra classes.

But this English teacher got under my skin. Our first assignment was to write a paper about our neighborhood. Now how was I gonna do that and keep my cover? Well, I was Black and he probably thought I was poor anyway—no need to lie. I'll just describe my neighborhood, using my best English. How he gon' circle the words "nocturnal insects"? I thought I was helping him understand how roaches rolled in the hood. He wrote just as much as I did, drew all kinds of red circles around my words.

Crossed out some of my best stuff! At the end of the ink was "Grade D/ Please make an appointment to see me."

It was my first office hour visit with a professor. "Hi, You gave me a D and said I should make an appointment, so how do I improve my grade?"

"Miss Richardson," said my young, blowhard, long-haired, laid back, lame, faded-jeans-wearing White dude English professor candidly. The look he shot me seemed to anticipate the answer to the rhetorical question: "What city school district are you from?"

"Cleveland," I said.

Flabbergasted, he shook his head and exhaled in a long loud breath that blew his bang back from his forehead. "Cleveland Public. Hmmm. Figures. You should work on each assignment in the writing center with the tutors. Did you bring the paper with you?"

Offended, "Yeah, I brought it," I replied in a stronger voice, as I sat down, reached in my book bag, dug out the paper and handed it to him. While he read and scratched his head, I began to plead. "Okay, this was the first assignment. I figured I could describe my neighborhood without no help. If you show me what to do, I can figure it out." I'm thinking, *I done been away from high school for six years, out in the world, conversing with doctors, lawyers, and men from all walks of life. I been using English (among other thangs) good enough to make hundreds of thousands of bucks and stay alive, and I need some square White folk to help me write about my hood? I don't think so.*

"Most students who take advantage of the writing center improve by at least one letter grade. I allow one revision, one extra week per paper. No guarantees. The tutor reports what you worked on and signs off on it. Got it?" He said with an air of arrogance as he looked up over his glasses and handed my paper back to me.

"Yeah, I got it."

My next stop was the Writing Center. All the tutors looked white and most of the clients were Asian, Black, and perhaps west side Puerto Ricans. Something was wrong with this picture, but what could I do? The young White girl assigned to work with me seemed nice enough.

"Tutors don't fix the paper. We read 'em over, offer suggestions and ask ya questions for clarification to assist with your writing goals. How zat sound?"

"Sounds great," I said in nasal-ish Northeast Ohio White girl speak.

She asked over and over about passages pertaining to nocturnal insects, after-hour joints, reefah spots, and number houses.

"Whadidya mean to say here?"

I looked her dead in her eyes and said, "I meant what I said."

Still confused, she asked, "Can you say this another way?"

Irritated, "If I have to. Maybe. Why?"

"Yer reader needs clarification."

"What you mean, my reader? It sounds clear to me. That don't sound clear to you?"

Time was up. I'm thinking, *What a waste!* Maybe she thought the same thing, but she said that I could sign up as often as I wanted but that I had to come at least once a week, and that between sessions, I should concentrate on rewriting some of the passages for clarity and precise expression. What the hell? I signed up again for the next available spot which was the next day.

When I returned, same tutor. Proud of my work, I showed her where I had revised the passages. She quickly read them over and asked me to read them aloud to her. Before I could complete a phrase, she kept stopping me after every other word.

"I don't know if I'm getting yer meaning. Do ya mind if I consult one of the other tutors?"

"Get whoever you want. Y'all the professionals."

"Great, It'll just be a few minutes."

After reviewing my paper with her co-worker a few minutes, another young lady comes over: "Looks like you reeal-ly got into the assignment. That's great."

"Thanks."

"Uhmmm... I think we should work on mechanics, punctuation and word choice. Things like that. How zat?"

"Okay." I'm like, *Whatevah*.

"See here. Every time you end an idea, you need a period. Now where does your idea end?"

"At the end."

Wrong again. Wherever she said an idea ended, I'd mark the period. Some of the words and phrases left unmarked by the professor in the original draft, she marked "awkward." Damn near everything I wrote was awkward let them tell it. Once again, as soon as we got going, time was up. I was relieved because most of her suggestions got on my damn nerves. I could tell by the look on her face that she really wasn't feelin the paper. I just made another appointment for the next day because I needed good grades to stay in school and I wasn't gonna let them run me out!

Next day same shit, different tutor. I caught on quick. Go along. Get along. Except, I wasn't lettin go of some of my words—including nocturnal insects!

I was still in "Special Studies," the college for remedial students. One of its benefits was also free tutoring, so I signed up with them too. My English tutor over there was this beautiful young Black woman. Now that was different. What was special about Special Studies was that their tutors were mostly people of color. At our first session, I handed over all of my paper drafts to her and explained that I really didn't understand why I got a D on it.

She read and giggled and pointed out particular phrases that she liked including the circled and crossed out "nocturnal insects." I knew right then, we were gonna get along. She read over some passages with me and said I should try to feel where commas and periods should go. Commas are like taking breaths, and periods are when you need to just stop, she said. I explained to her that I'd written in high school and junior high, although most writing there was fill in the blank worksheet type stuff, that I was in the vocational education track and wasn't expected to go to college, so they didn't teach me college writing. But even still, I had already taken a Developmental Reading and Developmental Writing course before I got kicked out of CSU. Those courses taught reading comprehension, "standard English grammar," and how to learn new vocabulary. I passed both of those courses with a satisfactory "S."

"They treat me like I'm illiterate!"

"Elaine, you have a strong voice and a nice way of expressing your ideas. They can't deal with your style, but don't let them kill your voice. You got a D on this paper, because your style is not in a college format. You're not illiterate. Ain't nothing wrong with your mind." Denise was more like a coach. Her attitude was like "get in there champ and give it your best shot!" She said I had my own style and a voice. I hadn't heard that before. Equipped with a faint sense of style, voice, hope and 2 or 3 rewrites, I still wound up getting a C from Mr. Long-haired laid- back lame white dude English professor. He couldn't feel me. And, I wasn't feelin him.

There was one other Black student in the class—Mike. We were around the same age and from the same kind of place. Mike was tall and skinny, a handsome light brown-skinned brotha, with freckles around his nose. He wore his hair in a bushy fro. Even before we communicated verbally with one another, I knew Mike and I were on the same page. Every time the prof made a statement based on the assumption that everyone saw the world the same way, we'd give each other Black folks' eye contact. I finally met Mike personally in the writing lab lobby: "This class is for the birds. This chump be trying to change what people are writin befoe he even knows what you tryna say."

"I know, he come givin me a D and makin me sign up for the writing center."

"This chump don't know nothin about Black folks. I was using *Manchild in the Promised Land* as my model, and he was trippin, crossin out every other word! These lil tutors in here, too. Please! I ain't even worried about it, sis. I got a wife and a family. My wife takes classes at night. We just need they little degrees so we can do what we got to do to take care of ourselves. Knowwhatumsayin?"

"Yes I do."

Doin what I had to meant that I had to play along with the unwritten liberal White rule that difference don't make a difference in education. It also meant I had to learn how to study, how to learn so that ideas made sense to me, how to study while managing my kids and going to AA meetings almost every night with Veronica.

Some of the stuff I was learning in AA was helping me deal with my classes and everyday life: "God, grant me the serenity to accept the things I cannot change, courage to change the things I can, and the wisdom to know the difference." "First things first." "Keep it Simple, Stupid."

I had to learn how to get up every morning, get my kids ready, get me ready, and get out of the house. I had to learn or relearn basics like how to use the library, how to use a computer, how to make my money and food stamps stretch to the end of the month, so I could have lunch money and bus fare. *Hongry*, my life depended on doin school. I wasn't going to college to fill other people's expectations anymore. School was all I had. I liked to read. And, in my earlier life, I had been a good student—at least by inner city school standards. But did I really have what it took to do college?

School English is a bitch! It looks you in the face and tells you, you don't even know what you know. But the deeper I looked into my daily school experiences and assignments, the more I realized that Mike and my young Black woman tutor, Denise, were right. We weren't illiterate as the prof and tutors made us out to be. They just didn't have a clue about Black folks. And they didn't see who we were or where we came from as an important part of the educational process. Each assignment we had in this Freshman English class told the story.

For our next assignment we were to analyze the essay "The Student as Nigger" by Jerry Farber and agree or disagree with its thesis. I raised my hand immediately after reading over the assignment and asked: "What do they mean by nigger, student, and what is a thesis?" The professor seemed disturbed that I did not know, but he opened up the questions for class discussion. A student explained that the author of the essay was comparing the experience of the average college student to the experience of Black people in America. Another student chimed in saying that just like slaves, students do not have a voice. Another answered that like slaves, students are taught to do as they are told whether it is to their own benefit or not. Another said he believed the author was saying that school teaches students to submit to authority. With every statement offered by these good students, me and Mike gave each other the "These white people kill me" look. Next, the prof asked the students to explain what a thesis statement was. He was pleased when they said it is the central argument of the essay that the author sets out to prove. I thought to myself, *How in the hell can the author prove that these whitebread students have been niggered? This is a joke.*

I already knew I was gonna disagree with each and every point the author made. This was surely gonna be an easy A paper for me. After class, I couldn't wait to talk to Mike. Just like I knew he would, Mike spoke victory words. "We bof gonna kick ass on this paper!" I couldn't wait to go to the computer lab to bust out my draft.

My next meeting with Denise, I showed her the assignment and my draft. She said I was definitely on the right track. She helped me set up my argument, my thesis, my little topic sentences and I ran it all down. I argued from personal experience. I had entered this class, this university and been told in so many words that I was illiterate because the words I used were *awkward*, not recognized as college format, because I didn't know how to punctuate sentences. I did not have the right words to describe my own neighborhood. I did not have a voice. Just as the professor told me in so many words during my first office visit, I was underprepared because I graduated from Cleveland Public schools. I was one of those "Where do they get these people from?" students. My mom went to the 6th grade and my dad to the 11th. I came from generations of hard working, non-formally educated people who did the best they could to survive in the ghettos of the world.

In my writing center trips, the tutors pass my paper around like so much jibber jabber. I grew up in a world where my image, my words, my life was not valued. Yeah, you right. I am a nigger and so is Mike. But these white students in this class be getting A's and B's because their writing is so perfect and in the right words and in the college format. They graduated from Shaker, Maple Heights, Cleveland Heights, Central Catholic, Benedictine, Euclid, Berea, Beaumont, privileged and private schools. And, they lived in safe suburbs or neighborhoods where they didn't have to be psychologically if not physically torn down every time they came outdoors. They knew next to nothing about struggle. I totally disagreed with Jerry Farber, the prof, the students, the whole shebang.

I revised that paper over and over. I couldn't wait to get my grade. When the day finally came, there was a note at the bottom of the paper, "Please visit my office hours." I couldn't believe it. I just knew I would have a big red "A." I couldn't wait to get Denise's opinion. She assured me that everything would be alright. When I went to the prof's office, he asked me how much of the paper I wrote by myself. *Huh? What kind of question is this?* I thought. *Yeah, I wrote it with my own mind.* I told him that Denise gave me input but she didn't write it.

"Well, your grade is a B-. Great improvement," he said with a smug grin.

I shot a fake grin back to him. Humiliated again, I couldn't wait to tell Denise. She hit the roof when I told her my grade and what he said.

"Elaine you can't let him talk to you like that. He thinks you can't think. Ain't nothing wrong with your mind. You're smart. He doesn't appreciate your ideas. I'm gonna go over there and tell him something. Who does he think he is?" And she did. One day after class, she was there waiting in the hall. She beckoned to the prof to come over to her and they exchanged words. She felt it was her duty to protect my voice. I didn't hear their conversation. When they finished she came over to me loudtalking saying, "You have good ideas and a nice way of expressing them. Don't let them kill your voice."

At our next class meeting, I asked Mike what he got. He started loudtalking saying, "He got the power in here, but I'll kick his punk ass outside." Mike never told me what he got, but I know he was not feelin it.

I wound up getting a C for the course. I was on my way to figuring out one reason that the White kids that we sat next to didn't get the same grades as people like Mike and me. That problem was a lot bigger than us. Not long after that I read a book by Carter G. Woodson, *The Miseducation of the Negro*. Dr. Woodson talked about the educational situation of Black people in the 1920s and 1930s—how Black people are taught to respect the oppressor's view of the world and our own oppression within it. There are so many obstacles that wound the spirit of Black students daily through teaching inappropriate or irrelevant content, and hurtful ways that we treat each other as humans. Add that together with keeping us poor and powerless and you get the so-called "achievement gap" and a host of other systems that keep us down.

A couple quarters passed and I was now working in the library at the reserve desk. One day, I noticed this older white-haired White man staring at me through wire framed glasses. He was a tall slender gentleman, with a kind smiling face that sported a long straight pointy nose. "May I help you?" I asked in genuine wonder.

"I remember you," he said.

My mind started racing—Oh Lord, who in the world is this old White man that knows me? A former customer? A retired vice cop? Who is this? And why is he talkin to me?

"I'm Jack Soules. And you're the A/F girl. You slept a lot in the front row of my Physics course a few years back, remember? Too much partying, does it every time. You got an F on the midterm, and then managed to get an A on the final and a C for the course. I never forget a bright student. So, are you ready for college now?"

"I hope so," I answered with a sigh of relief.

"We need bright Black students like you in Physics. What's your major?"

Major? I had struggled through a couple of English classes. I wasn't that good in anything. Dr. Soules said that if I ever needed help I should come see him for any subject. Wow! I had an actual professor, a seemingly cool White man, offering to tutor me! Of all the students he'd taught, he remembered me. Life is a funny thang! I didn't know if I would take him up on it. I just put it on a shelf in my brain.

By this time, I was taking an English course called Writing about Literature. The professor of the course was rigid, to say the least. He was an Ivy Leaguer. If he wasn't, he surely could have been. He was Jewish and serious as a heart attack. He always wore dark dress suits, shirts, and ties to every class that complimented his strictness. His hair always parted over to the right side and his black rimmed glasses gave him a square, 1940s look. On the first day of class, he passed out a hefty syllabus and a set of rules called "Seven Deadly Sins." One of the rules was *Do not use "like" when you mean "as."* **Example: Winston tastes good like a cigarette should.** *This is poor usage.*

After the first class meeting, the class size dropped enormously. If I thought I had been humiliated about my writing before, I hadn't seen nuthin yet. One thing about this prof though, he was an equal opportunity slasher. When I went to his office hours, he'd have White boys coming out of his office with tears in they eyes. I even heard one curse him out! The comments I got back from him were designed to degrade: "Have you ever heard of the dictionary?" "Have you ever heard of a comma?" "This paper rambles." "Poor usage." "Dialectal variant." And of course, the standard: "*awkward.*" He knew damned well I knew what a dictionary and a comma was, but those questions were beside the point. I felt like he wanted to insult my intelligence more than help me spell out my ideas or strengthen my readings of the literary works he assigned. More than severe, his comments cut wildly, with him seemingly giving less than a damn about whether his feedback helped students become better writers or sent them home depressed, nervous, angry or all three.

The one thing I didn't know about was dialectal variant. What the hell was that? Professor Rigid broke it down to me.

"Miss Richardson, when your prose breaks down its because your logic has broken down...syntax problems come up not just when someone doesn't have a command of the language or grammar, but because he or she hasn't thought the argument through carefully enough. The language from your home and neighborhood is fine in that context, but it doesn't work for the kind of careful analysis and expression expected in academic writing."

I still didn't know what the hell he was talkin about. And he didn't know what I was talkin about. I decided I would visit Dr. Soules' office, take him up on his offer to help me, to see if he could make me understand Dr. Rigid. Doc Soules said that I tended to drop into Black dialect, that I should try to write more like I talked. I code switched when I was trying to project a positive self-image, especially when speaking to White folks. My mama taught me that. I knew White folks thought you were dumb if you sounded Black. So, for Dr. Rigid, Black words in my writing meant sloppy logic, weak analysis and poor expression. Something about that didn't sit right with me. I knew how to disagree with an author, and I had good reasons for interpreting a story or a poem the way I did, but because I did it in my own style, my point of view was degraded. I could hear Denise's Black woman's voice in the back of my mind, "Don't let them kill your voice." In my visits to Dr. Rigid's office hours, I began to question him about my words, my sentences, my ideas and how I put them together—my voice. Some of the stuff he taught me, I agreed with and some of it I didn't.

I worked beyond hard in Rigid's class. Between Doc Soules, Denise, the Writing Center and Rigid's office hours, I managed to pull a B in the course. Rigid was so well known for weeding out the weary, especially "minority," students, that word spread of my grade. I was among the few Black people in CSU's folklore to earn a B from him. Shortly after, Mr. Brownlowe, who had a rep for being no-nonsense and mean, the director of Special

Studies, offered me a position as a tutor. Up until this point, the only courses that I had ever gotten a B in were Black American History from 1877 and Introduction to Urban Studies. I started to gain confidence in my academic abilities. I declared English as my major and Secondary Education as my minor. I didn't know what I could do with an English major. But I was beginning to like writing, and I figured if I could get a B from Rigid, I was more than a conqueror.

There was only one Black woman in the English department around this time and she was a linguistics professor. I couldn't wait to take her class: The Elements of Linguistics. She was a very attractive cocoa brown-skinned middle-aged woman with salt and pepper hair, a keen face, with cute dimples and a very nice smile. I didn't know anything about her before I took her class. It became obvious to me very quickly that she was one of those professors who strove to avoid issues of power and diversity in language when we got to the study of so-called dialect. She tried to teach linguistics as though it was neutral. The question *Who gets to call what anyone speaks a language or a dialect?* was never called. She tried very hard to avoid contact with Black students. She almost jumped out of her skin one day when I tried to speak to her after class. I still learned a lot from her and earned a B in the course.

Not long after taking her class, the English department hired another Black woman professor and her specialty was Black literature. I had taken one other Black literature course before but the professor did not have a command of the subject. Not that a White professor can't be an excellent teacher of Black literature, but it was clear that it was not her area of expertise and she was just filling in until CSU hired an expert. The new Black woman professor was surely an expert. She knew not only the literature, she was well versed in the history and complicated culture of Black Americans. I had my doubts at first because she was *trea'in fe white*, but I found out pretty quickly that she was, without a doubt, culturally Black. In her class, I was introduced to Langston Hughes, Ann Petry, Jean Toomer, Zora Neale Hurston, James Weldon Johnson, Chester Himes, Claude McKay, Margaret Walker and many other important Black writers who helped create the Black literary tradition. I learned about the Buffalo Soldiers, A. Philip Randolph and The Pullman Porters, and much more. She taught me that it was important to understand Black culture in order to understand our literature. One day after we got to know each other, I confessed to her that I was a former streetgirl.

She asked me what took me so long to figure out I had a brain! What I failed to tell her was street people have brains. It's just that we get caught up using them for the underground economy.

The most important thing I learned from Professor Gosselin was "Never judge a book by its cover." I earned a B in her class, too.

Another course that made a huge impression on me was Urban Language Patterns. It was taught by the Director of Black Studies, Dr. Mims, who was also a Speech Language professor. Dr. Mims' class was all about how Black and inner city folks use language. The class was geared toward future educators. One of our assigned readings especially peaked my interest: "English Teacher Why You Be Doin the Thangs You Don't Do" by Geneva Smitherman. The writer talked about the very experience I was having in college English courses. Instead of teaching me how to write with power, to develop my voice, to analyze arguments, to become a critical thinker, instructors and tutors concentrated on "cleaning up" my grammar and correct punctuation.

Smitherman said that teachers should use improvisational drama, discussions, debates, short speeches to develop the verbal gifts that Black students already have. She also recommended that teachers teach students to study dialects and the relationship between language and power. One of the points she made that I always thought but had never seen in writing was that language is another thing used to oppress Black and poor people, and that people from the ghetto are made to feel that their language isn't worth anything. She said teachers should focus on improving the reading ability of Black students, and teachers should help students focus on getting their message across with power and clarity. I mean she was saying stuff in that article that stuck with me. To top it all off she laced the article with Black language! Yeah, bring out the powerful voices, ideas and thoughts of Black youth. Blam!

I started looking up everything I could find with her name on it. Her book, *Talkin and Testifyin: The Language of Black America* spoke to my spirit. Black people's ways of talking was not sloppy, broken, or a bunch of mistakes. Our language styles began in West African language styles. When our various "masters" forced our ancestors to take on their languages in the Caribbean, the Americas, or Europe we gave those languages a serious make-over and made them fit us!

Wow! How come nobody ever taught us this? My previous education kept me in the dark on my language. If you don't feel good about your language or value it, you can't possibly feel good about yourself. Your language is your heart, your brain, your family, your history. It was the first time that I read or even heard somewhere that what Black people spoke was a treasure, that its history was respectable, that Black language is not just slang, foul language, and street talk. I learned that Black language is a part of African American culture. I always thought deep inside that I was smart, that my Mama and Daddy and family were smart, or at least, not dumb, and Smitherman's book confirmed it for me. When I found out that I could study Black people and our languages and ways of talking—*Blam*! It was on! I became a double major in English and Applied Linguistics. It got to the point where I knew more about the history of African Americans and language than anyone on campus. Doc Soules informed me that I even became the topic of conversation a few times at some of the good ole boys' bridge games.

I'm not a quitter. When I put my mind to something, I work at it with all my might. When I wasn't at school or work, I'd work for hours in my dining room on the desktop computer that Mama bought for me on her May Company charge account. It took Mama a long time, but she finally saved enough to buy a duplex and I lived downstairs. If the girls started swinging from the chandeliers, I could tell them to go upstairs to my parents' apartment, or I could send them to Tauntie's, who loved them just as much as we did. When I needed a break I'd turn on the TV just to refuel. One day while taking a break, a breaking news story caught my attention: "Prostitute fatally shot in parking lot at East 75th and Chester Avenue. News at 5:00."

"75th and Chester.... Damn, I wonder who that was?"

Maybe it was some new chick from outta town. I hope it ain't nobody I know. The 5:00 o'clock news took 2 years to come on. When they finally reached that segment of the news, I saw Queen Bee and some of my other ex-coworkers talking to the investigators saying that Candy turned a date with this cop and he came back later, laid in the cut and shot her. He was angry because she beat him for his wallet.

"Oh God, it's Candy, it's Candy, oh my God. He didn't have to kill her. I told her to stop takin niggas' wallets," I sobbed off and on for days.

I wish Candy could have made it off the streets. She had a daughter. She was a nice girl. He didn't have to kill her. Why do people think that girls caught up in prostitution deserve to die when selling sex is part of America's gross national product? Is it really hard out here for a pimp? Prostitutes are sisters, daughters, mothers, wives, lovers, friends, and children! Not to mention husbands, fathers, and sons. Human trafficking is human trafficking. People write poor folks off, especially, poor Black streetgirls. We get dogged out, like we were born to be hoes and we love it, after all we chose to be with pimps. But did we really? Did we really choose trauma? We make what I call trauma-induced choices. Even if we are blessed to recover we may never be able to live down the label.

They say you cain't turn a ho into a housewife. In the movie playing in my head, I was the leading lady and wife; housewife, maybe not, but wife, yes. I didn't want to come within one inch of a pimp. I always wanted to be a wife. My mama was married. I had a father, and I wanted one for my girls. Although I was still young, I was older than many of the students I took classes with and I never met any brothas my age I could feel the magic for.

I was the queen of stigma: ex-prostitute, ex-drug addict, hood-dweller, baby mama of two "illegitimate" children. I needed a man strong enough to deal with my past without me covering it up. A neighborhood friend kept tellin me about this fine single brotha she knew. She set it up so that Calvin and I finally got a chance to meet—he was as good lookin and hard workin as she said he was. He was a few years younger than me. He worked in heating and cooling and construction. He had that hard man fit physique, kinda thick but not overweight, smooth brown skin, fine curly jet black hair, brilliant smile with a slight gap in his front teeth. His hands were harsh, like he grew up hammering, hauling, and hoisting. His everyday dress was t-shirts, blue jeans or jogging pants and a cut off sweatshirt. When we went out, he wore nice jewelry and nice leisure suits. He was sexy. His background was squeaky clean, and he seemed like a level-headed and wise gent.

On our first date, he took me to a car show. It felt good to have someone hold my hand, put his big strong arms around me, open doors for me, take me out, cook for me, not expect sex or anything except companionship. Calvin also did a lot of work on my apartment. He installed ceiling fans, did drywall, repaired my furnace. He helped me as much as he could. I told Calvin all about my past. He said it didn't matter and he could deal with it. He was everything I thought I needed. Right around the same time I started dating Calvin, I met another good lookin hard workin brother.

Tall, slim, cocoa brown, and cute, Chris had perfect white teeth. Nice face and soft skin. His hair was fine, jet black and curly just like Calvin's. He had long soft fingers and hands. His jeans were always neatly pressed and he was always well-dressed. Although I'd always been a sucker for a fine brotha, I was beyond being attracted to a guy solely on good looks. Chris was very interesting and ambitious. He worked in the library at CSU, while working on his undergraduate degree in business. Like Calvin, he was younger than me. Every time we ran into each other in the library or around campus, he'd compliment me on my hair, my dress, my smile. We always had pleasant informative or innocent flirty chats when we saw each other in passing. He asked me out a couple times, but I never took him up on it because I was involved with Calvin. Plus though he seemed genuinely attracted to me, he had that playboy look about him, like he had plenty women, like he was far from ready to be steady, so I wasn't sweatin him.

Almost a year into our relationship, Calvin confessed to me that he was involved with another woman, that she was pregnant by him, and he wanted to do the right thing. He said that he had decided to move to Atlanta to be with her and to raise their child. I was totally crushed. I loved being intimate with him. When we got together it was magic. He was the first man whose company I truly enjoyed. And as far as sex, we made love. None of that wham bam I please you and that's it shit. Nah. Calvin was a lover. How could he cheat on me? Deep inside, I felt that the reason he chose this woman over me was because of my past. My self-esteem was not high enough for me to overcome the disappointment. In the past, when people hurt me, I used dope to cope. I knew what I would do to get over his ass.

The next time I saw Chris in the library, I flirted back with him and asked him if he still wanted to take me out. I told myself that I didn't care about Calvin. "Go on with your woman to Atlanta. I ain't gone let no square ass nigga play me." Chris and I linked up under stupid pretenses. I needed to rebound and though I wanted more, I accepted what he had to offer...sex. We only went on one or two real dates. He didn't put much effort into escalating our friendship. We had a bootie call type relationship.

He was there for me and I was there for him. It was just something for both of us to do. Almost every time we did it, I wished I was with Calvin. He probably felt the same way, wishing I was some other girl.

In just a few short months, to my surprise, Calvin moved back to Cleveland. He come callin me one day talkin bout he made a mistake, that he shouldn't have broke it off with me, that he wanted us to try it again. When we got back together we picked up right where we left off. To my surprise, I still loved him, and I wanted to accelerate my plan of being a wife. I decided I would get pregnant by him. Afterall, he had left me to "do the right thing" with another woman. If I got pregnant, surely, he would "do the right thing" and raise our child together. Mind you, although I was in my last year of undergraduate studies, I didn't know what my future held as far as financial security. I was still on welfare. But I just figured everything would work itself out.

I put my plan into action. Calvin was always careful as far as condom use. I had to figure out how to make it come off and for him to notice that he ejaculated inside of me. I got my chance and worked my plan. Every time we were intimate, I used my hand to pull him out each time I felt he was about to reach a climax. Each time I pulled him out, I worked the condom ever so slightly until I got it off and locked my hips around him in such a way that he couldn't help but to have an orgasm. "Oops, baby, the condom came off," I would say. "Damn girl, we have to be careful. We ain't ready for no more kids." *You ain't ready for no more, I am.*

Sure enough, in a few weeks, I was pregnant. I couldn't wait to tell Calvin. Although he didn't jump for joy as I hoped he would, at least he asked me if I was sure he was the father, instead of the reply that I had heard the other times in my life from other guys—"It ain't none of mines."

•13•

Graduation

HOW DO YOU ANNOUNCE your third child when you're an underemployed unwed undergraduate student?

"Mama, I'm having another baby."

"Jeezus Cryse, is fe Calvin?"

"Yes, Mama, who else?"

I didn't tell anybody else. I let the lump in my blouse do the work. My brother, hit the ceiling.

"How many babies do you need to have to prove that you a real woman? You a real woman. You a real woman. Does that do it for you? Don't be one of them chicks that have a trail a crumbs. Ain't no brotha that's about somethin gonna wanna be with you. You betta hope Calvin stick witchu."

That stuck in my head. Would Calvin ask me to marry him? Would I ask him? I was afraid of his answer. Why would anybody wanna marry me? Although we *been* out of the stone ages, a poor Black woman with a big belly and no ring on her finger is still called a baby mama or a ho. I made up my mind. Okay, I gotcho baby mama and ya ho. Gettin my degree was the only way I could tell the world to kiss where the sun don't shine. I had a good support system for my girls. Between Mama, my play Godmama, Tauntie, my tutor, Denise and her family, Veronica, Doc Soules, Dr. Edwards, and my church. I had my cheering section, rootin me on.

To my surprise everyone seemed a little nicer to me when my belly got big—well not everyone, them welfare caseworkers always acted like they were better than people. But as far as school went, while workin in the tutoring center and the library and taking classes, people seemed to go out of their way to be nice to me, even my boss in the tutoring center, Mr. Brownlowe. In my 9th month, he kept telling me to stay home. Every time he saw me at work, he'd say, "Doggone, we believe in putting your education first, but we don't want you to have that baby here. Girl, don't you come back here to work next week." He was so close to right. On our last day of work before winter break, Mr. Brownlowe gave a Christmas party for us—John, Denise, Robert, Martin, Stan the Man, and me. I had so much fun. We played music, told jokes, played hangman. I ate everything on the menu—scholarly party foods, veggies and dip, brie cheese and crackers, hummus. Stuff I would have turned my nose up at in earlier days. Lord, but I did dance, big belly and all!

That evening when I got home, my back began to ache. At first, I didn't pay it any attention, but soon, I realized that I was in labor! I called Calvin and told him that I thought I was ready to have the baby. "Mommy gone have the baybee," "Mommy gone have the baybee," my daughters danced and sang joyfully. They wanted to come to the hospital with us, but when Calvin got to my house, we gave the girls to Tauntie as we rushed to Metro General. Every pothole we hit seemed to get me a percentage of a centimeter closer to delivery. Calvin must have asked me a thousand times if I was alright. After forever and a day, we arrived at the hospital. Somebody put his hand down there and announced that I was totally dilated! Doctors, nurses, midwives rushed into position. "Elaine, do not push until we are ready."

"Well, whoooo, the baby…whoooo…is ready," I said as I pushed but tried not to in slow anguish.

"It's comin!" Calvin warned me as he held my hand.

"It's comin out," I whispered.

"It's a girl! Congratulations mom and dad!" somebody said.

I didn't know babies could be born so fast. Calvin saw everything. He stayed there with me after the baby was born. He held her, looked at her fingers, her hair, her feet, her pretty little face. It was the first time I thought a guy was there for me. Fast as the baby came Calvin was gone. The Christmas season of 1990 was still the best I ever had. I dropped that load and was back in school the next quarter.

Spring quarter 1991 was my last quarter of undergrad. Things seemed so hectic. Sometiems I had to leave the baby in a basket in the tutoring center and ask someone to watch her in between classes. Even Mr. Brownlowe watched her one time when my childcare arrangements fell through.

I had worked a lot on career exploration. With all my training and interests, I was sure I'd make a great high school English teacher. I signed up for the Ohio Education Job Fair at CSU. School districts from all over the state came to campus to interview CSU's newly minted pre-service teachers. I was armed with wisdom from a very courageous sister by the name of Henia. She'd started a group that focused on helping ex-offenders transition to society.

One of her main directives to us was to never lie on a job application. She knew the consequences first hand. After working her way off the streets, overcoming a felony conviction and obtaining a professional career, she was fired when the company she worked for was sold to new owners, who ran a background check on her and found that she'd never disclosed her felony conviction. Well, I'd never have to worry about lying on any application, since I never had a felony. You couldn't tell me, I wasn't the one to watch.

I had my stereotypical clean-cut teacher-look down pat. Navy blue business suit, starched ivory white blouse, well-shined navy blue patent leathers. I flashed my credentials at every district's station—Standardized Academic American English, applied linguistics, writing tutor, African American literature specialization, British and American literature experience, excellent results with diverse student populations, great practicum experiences at inner city and suburban schools—Jane Addams and Cleveland Heights High. The offers would just be overflowing. To my surprise, every application I read asked a question I wasn't ready to answer: "Have you ever been arrested?" Arrested? What about have you ever been convicted of a felony?

Damn! I didn't wanna have to explain to school administrators that I had worked the streets and that I had been arrested over 200 times. They might think I was a sexual pervert, a pedophiliac, or that I would corrupt minors. I couldn't really fault the school districts for being extra careful about the adults they allow to work with youth. I walked my navy blue business suit to the bus stop, caught the bus and went home, not knowing what I would do. Neither Career Services nor Henia's group prepared me for that! I just told myself over and over that God wouldn't let me be one of those people you hear about with a college degree workin fries at Mickey D's.

The next day at school, I ran into my friend, John, a very cool long pony tail and eye glass wearing white boy, fellow English major and a damn good poet. He always had my back. If I had to miss class, he'd give me the notes and fill me in on lectures. We both worked together as tutors in the writing center and for Special Studies.

"E, how was the job fair?"

"It didn't really work out for me. Sheeit. Every school that I wanted to apply to had a question on their application askin about any and all arrests. And you know about my record."

"Bummer... . I applied for a graduate assistantship, you should, too."

"What's that?"

"Apply for the Master's in English program and let them know that you wanna be considered for a grad assistantship. If you get the assistantship you get to teach freshman writing or work in the writing center and the department pays your tuition in exchange, plus you get a stipend. If you get your Master's Degree, you can be a college English instructor and work with adults. That way your past record might not be so much of a problem. You should go for it."

"Wow, you think they'd take me?"

"Elaine, you are one of the smartest people here and they need qualified Black TAs. You'll get in."

I didn't have anything to lose. I went straight to the English department and applied just barely getting my paperwork in before the deadline. I needed letters of recommendation. My references? Dr. Rigid and Mr. Brownlowe! With them on my side I was a serious contender. A few days later, booyahkah! Yeah, I was accepted into the Master's program and awarded an assistantship.

I was really graduating and accepted into a Master's program. My family was so proud of me. Mama's friends, coworkers, people from near and far dropped by the house, day in and day out. My Uncle Fred, Aunt Sweets and Cousin Arlene came from New York to be with us. My good fortune was the center of celebration by all who visited or called the Richardson's residence for at least a month. It was almost like a Jamaican wake.

One day, during the summer of my undergrad graduation, he knocked on my door. I hadn't seen my oldest daughter's father in years. I had heard that he had been in jail, that he was out and lookin for me. I had graduated from the smooth talk, good looks and streetlife swagger that had me shook years before. An interaction between us would be... would be... *awkward*. We didn't have anything in common except our child. I had never asked him for anything. I couldn't. He never offered anything. He couldn't. He never worked a legit job his whole life that I knew of. The only thing I ever knew him to do was live off women. What could he possibly want? I looked through the peephole and saw him standing there. By chance, Calvin was there with us that day. I told him who was at the door and he answered it:

"S'up. Yeah, I came to see my kid."

"Oh, okay. Did you call Elaine? Yo, man, you need to call before you drop by. I have a child with Elaine, too, and me and mines be here, so you need to work out your arrangements, man. She got your numba?"

"She know how to get in touch with me through my family."

"Cool."

"Oh, it's like dat, huh?"

"Yeah, it's like dat."

Mack used to be a terrorist! I was surprised that it went down so smooth.

When I finally did get his phone number, so he could talk to our daughter, he talked to her out of anger, asking my little child why she never came to visit him in the penitentiary. He complained to her that "Your mama broke the bloodline, by havin a baby by anotha nigga." She was an innocent little kid. While I never told my girls anything bad about him, I did tell them that I had worked the streets and I lied to them both at first, telling my oldest and my middle daughters that Mack was their father. But when my middle daughter got older, I told her the truth—that I didn't know who her father was. That I had gotten so high one night that I became careless and that I knew what her father looked like, but I didn't know how to get in touch with him. I never wanted anybody to be able to hurt my girls and throw in their face that their mama useta be a ho.

As my oldest daughter got older, she was able to make sense of the situation for herself. Not only did I allow her to contact Mack, I allowed her to know her brother and her sister that Mack had by former wife-in-laws. You can say that my oldest daughter's relationship with her father is… *awkward*.

I knew what I would write my Master's thesis on the day I entered the program. I found something I loved, learning about Black people, language and literacy. My newfound interest made me love riding the bus and listening to people talk. Checkin out how College educated Black folks code switched in White company and code switched back to Black talk in Black company—or not. How some Black people didn't "sound Black." There is nothing more interesting to me than people and how they deal with each other in this crazy beautiful place we call the world!

A new fire was lit by every new idea I learned about how Black writers came to honor their own minds, styles and voices, that I wanted my children to learn about them, too. Language, writing, culture and history. We separate these to teach writing and language but they are really not that easy to untangle. At night, when I wasn't stressed working on a project, I'd read to the girls: *The Autobiography of Malcolm X*; *Incidents in the Life of a Slave Girl*; *Narrative of the Life of Frederick Douglass*; *The Interesting Narrative of the Life of Olaudah Equiano or Gustavus Vassa, The African: Written by Himself*.... I also found out about a wonderful opportunity for my girls—Mali Yetu. It means Our Wealth. Mali Yetu is an independent Afrocentric summer school for youth started by Black parents in Cleveland that focused on passing on the knowledge of Black culture and history to the youth. I found out about it after taking a class from Professor Sanza Clark on the Social Foundations of Education. I learned just as much about Black culture and history as a Mali Yetu parent as I did as a college student!

I also learned a lot from Dr. Mims' Black Studies speakers' series. He always invited dynamic and inspirational people to campus. I got to hear Dr. Molefi Asante (who developed the theory of Afrocentricity). He taught us that we must look at ourselves from our own perspective and to create our own knowledge. I was exposed to Dr. Maulana Karenga (the creator of Kwaanza), and Malcolm X's daughter, Sister Attallah Shabazz. But Dr. Mims brought one special speaker to campus that changed my life—Dr. Geneva Smitherman. In the weeks leading up to her lecture on "The Language of Black Americans: Be Who You Is," I was so excited. I couldn't wait to hear her speak and to ask her questions.

The day finally came. Her talk was da bomb! It was the first time, I saw a strikingly beautiful statuesque Black woman speak with such authority and versatility. She was raised by her Baptist preacher dad in the Black church, so she began her talk in that style. "First giving honor to God who's the head of my life, my ancestors in Africa, the Americas, and throughout the diaspora who survived the Holocaust of Enslavement... ." This was a sister who was creating new scholarship and showing what Black scholars could do. She switched up her style, remixing scholarship that recorded the voices of formerly enslaved Black people, contemporary boyz and girlz in da hood, older and middle-aged African American community folk, professionals, preachers, politicians, with academic talk.

She was Harriet Tubman, Sojourner Truth, Dr. Maya Angelou, Sister Souljah, Zora Neale Hurston, and the first Black woman linguist, originally from Jamaica, Dr. Beryl Bailey, all wrapped up into one. After her talk, no one had questions for her, except me. The rest of the audience was...speechless. I tried to ask her every question under the sun about her work and the question of African Americans, our ways of talking and literacy education.

At that point in my academics, I was stuck on the question of dialect: "Yes, I really enjoyed your lecture Dr. Smitherman. Thank you so much for coming to Cleveland. Does the first language or so-called dialect that a person learns stop them from learning another language or dialect? No known research has given an unqualified yes... ."

I was no longer the shaky slave with no self-confidence that I was when I entered CSU. After I asked my question, I looked into the blank stares of the audience. No one else had a question that they could voice. Were they stunned by the content? Turned off because she was celebrating and elevating the language of Black people to a science? Or, were the students just simply there for extra credit or campus activity points?

Although I cared, in that moment I cared more that God sent her there for me. At the reception that was held for Dr. Smitherman in the Black Cultural Center, only a few people came to shake her hand, introduce themselves, or to have their books signed. I had her all to myself!

"GeeNeeva, I want to introduce you to Elaine Richardson, she's one of our best students," bragged Dr. Mims.

"You can call me, Dr. G. How you doin girl?"

"Oh my goodness, I read everything I could find with your name on it," I said in utter admiration.

I mean, I was her disciple. Her work got me through undergrad and was influencing my thinking about my thesis. I started shooting off questions like there was no tomorrow. I was especially interested in the story she wrote about in *Talkin and Testifyin* of being denied a teaching license until she took a speech correction class. I mean, how could such a brilliant sista be discriminated against? We solved all the problems of educational bias against Black language speakers in twenty minutes!

"Girl, you done read all my stuff. Are you grad?"

"Yes, I'm in the Master's program in English, with a specialization in Composition and Applied Linguistics."

"What kind of grades do you have? You betta come on up here and get your Ph.D."

By this time, I was getting A's left and right. "Wooah, my grades are excellent but I don't know nothing bout no Ph.D."

She said it like she was asking me if I wanted a piece of sweet potato pie or if I wanted to be Denzel Washington's wife. I hadn't thought about getting a doctorate. I just wanted to get off welfare, teach school or something, get a regular paycheck every week or two, but a Ph.D.... .

"You think they uh gimme one?"

"Ain't nobody gone give you nuthin. You gotta work yo butt off for it. You take the GRE?"

"No."

"Take the GRE, apply to the doctoral program in English at Michigan State University."

"Wow, you think I can get in?"

"If you have strong credentials, you might get a university fellowship. First step though is that GRE. As far as my program, I can get you in. I direct the African American Language and Literacy program. Just do what I tell you to do."

"Wow, that's what's up."

Dr. G gave me her card and told me to stay in touch with her. I never dreamed this would happen. It was the meeting of preparation and opportunity.

I did exactly what Dr. G told me to do. I took the GRE, more than once to try to improve my scores. I kept in close contact with Dr. G. sharing my ideas and how I would design the research for my thesis. She liked my ideas. In fact, she laid the groundwork for the type of research I was interested in doing. Good thing, too, because Dr. Mims and I started having different ideas about my thesis. Dr. Mims did work on African American Language from a speech perspective. He understood it to be a system and not mistakes, but he didn't see how learning about it could work with literacy learning. Similarly, another English professor and linguist on my committee agreed with Dr. Mims, that I should take my thesis in another more "fruitful" direction.

I was so preoccupied around this time with my studies, that I wasn't as deeply involved in AA meetings anymore. I found out that my sponsor, Veronica, had a relapse. How could this be? She was my role model of how a street person could go straight and still be cool. My friend Gene told me that Veronica was back on Kinsman, running dope for people and getting drunk. Where was her son? Who was looking out for her? I was devastated. I made plans to find her. It wasn't hard. Kinsman was her stomping grounds.

"Hey, you seen Veronica?" I asked and asked, until somebody showed me where she was crashing, with some bad news dude she was stayin with in his mom's crib.

I walked up the stairs of a dingy narrow hallway on 130th and Kinsman. I gave four or five Po-leece knocks until I heard someone slowly creep closer and closer to the door. Finally, an elderly woman's voice creaked, "Who is it?"

"Hi, I'm lookin for my cousin, Veronica. I wanna see her. Please let me in."

After undoing 5 or 6 deadbolt locks, a bent over, darkskinned, skinny old lady, wearing an old lady housecoat and a scarf tied half way around her head, opened the door. A scent of cigarette-butt-filled astrays, Wild Irish Rose, dirty dishwater, and piss rushed up my nostrils.

"Thanks, where is she?" I said trying to sound calm and cool.

"She back there sleep. You ain't gon' be able to git no sense outta her. Gon' back there, you'll see her."

I found her in a deep stupor sleep, fully dressed. "Veronica, it's me, Elaine. Look." I might as well have been talking to a steel door. I shook her. Softly at first, but with more and more conviction as my voice grew louder.

"Veronica, I came to take you away from here. You gotta get up and get out of here. I got a car waiting outside. Don't worry bout bringing nothin. Let's just go."

"Huh." She lay there sluggishly, not budgin and not studyin about nuthin I was sayin. Her pretty hair all unkempt and matted against her scull, as in days of old. After a while of beggin and botherin her and not lettin her fall back into her drunken sleep, she looked me dead in the eye and said, "I ain't ready yet. I'll be ah-ight. Leave me yo phone numba."

"I don't wanna leave you here," my voice quivered.

"I'ma be ah-ight. You just keep goin ta school," she said with a slight smile, as she turned over and continued to try to get her snooze on.

I wrote my number down and left it on the nightstand next to the bed feeling helpless.

"I tole you. You wadn't gon' git no sense out of her," the old lady said to me as I walked outta the apartment.

But Veronica always made sense. I had no idea that would be my last time seeing her alive. Maybe she did.

I called her sponsor, Betty M., and told her what happened. She chewed me out, scolding me for being careless and foolish, for going into a place looking to bring her or anybody else out. She said I could have been beaten or worse. A few short weeks later, Veronica was dead. I guess she was drunk and stumbled out in front of a speeding truck on the corner of 134th and Kinsman. She was my friend. God put her in my path to show me that I could be a respectable sober woman, still be cool, and be a good mom, and then she was gone, showing me what might happen to me if I didn't "Just keep goin ta school."

I felt like I would die, if I failed at school. I was struggling to get my committee to buy into my ideas about language and literacy and Ted shows up like a breath of fresh air. Patient. Genuinely interested. That was Ted—the cutest, coolest, youngest White guy professor that I'd ever seen. He had just graduated from the University of Michigan's English Education program and had done his dissertation research on the Ann Arbor 1979 "Black English" case. I couldn't believe it. Kindred spirit. It's a done deal. I made Ted the head of my committee—or maybe God did. Not only did I have Ted, a "radical" white woman professor was appointed to my committee as an outside reader. I didn't even know how the stars were all being lined up for me.

I had never worked so hard on anything. I slept and ate my thesis. My project was about a young Black woman student's paper and her use of Black Talk. In it, I found many examples of Black Oral Tradition, sayings and pieces of folk wisdom that have stood the test of time and have helped Black people make it through this world. Her style of writing was similar to mine, a style overlooked and dismissed as *awkward*, not valued as culture, experience and knowledge.

I read many many books and articles on Black language, culture, applied linguistics and composition theory. One thing that frustrated me was that of all the readings, none seemed to really get at what I saw in this young woman's writing, my own and other Black students' writings. The only research that I read that came close was published by some researchers at Brooklyn College. The created a program called SEEK, which stands for Search for Education and Elevation through Knowledge. These researchers developed a curriculum that made Black language and culture the center of study in language and literacy education.

It is difficult to do something new when you are learning how to be a scholar. You have to convince your professors that what you are writing makes sense. Ted was right there for me. His style was non-threatening and supportive. He just asked me lots of questions and gave me scholarly ideas to challenge. "What do you think about this?" "Read this and tell me what you think."

I thought to myself, *If the Lord let's me graduate, don't nobody nowhere have to never worry about me writing nothing else about Black folks, language and literacy!* I must have revised, rewritten and re-everythanged that thesis at least 50 times! Even still, I was nervous because Ted was also a newbie, a brand new assistant professor. Would he have the juice to convince my other committee members that my work was not wrongheaded and that I deserved to be awarded a Master of Arts in English?

The day of my thesis defense finally arrived. A defense is when your committee, after having read your manuscript, asks you questions about your ideas, and you have to defend them. It is truly you defending and supporting your ideas orally. I believed in my work. I knew what I had communicated in my writing was representative of a lot of Black people's experiences with literacy education, but could I make them feel me? This must have been a little of how Phillis Wheatley felt back in the late 1700s when her white owners, the Wheatleys of Boston, and a group of well-respected Bostonians examined her about her book of poems. The Wheatley's supported Ms. Phillis Wheatley in her literacy education as a kind of experiment to see if Africans were the intellectual equals of Europeans. Ms. Phillis Wheatley was the first African American to have a book of poems published officially with the London publication of her *Poems on Various Subjects, Religious and Moral*. Phillis Wheatley passed her defense in flying colors, so to speak—and with the help of Dr. Ted Lardner and all of the scholars I learned from, so did I!

In 1991, I graduated from Cleveland State University with a Master of Arts in English, and I was awarded a Minority Competitive Doctoral Fellowship to attend Michigan State University. This fellowship meant that I did not have to pay one dime to earn my Ph.D. It was an affirmative action scholarship. But don't get it twisted. I was highly qualified—and like Dr. G explained to me, "You might get into a university on affirmative action, but you can't get out on it. You have to work your butt off!" I was in for the ride of my life! I packed up two of my daughters and off to East Lansing we went.

•14•
The Ph.D.

I'M HERE AT A world-class university. My children are living with me on campus in graduate family housing with people from all over the world. The world is much larger than I ever imagined, and my girls and I have access to it through our brains, hearts and hopes. We inherited this opportunity from our ancestors who lived, died, prayed, marched, and fought against all odds.

I started to realize my life as a kind of relay race. Grandma carried within her a great force. She was powerful in the spiritual realm. I wouldn't be where I am now, if it weren't for that ole Jamaican lady. She passed the baton of her beliefs, intellect, hard work, and ambition to Mama. Even though I ran off course, somewhere deep inside of me was a piece of the baton, a branch of the shame chree planted in me by Mama, guarded by Grandma in the spirit world: "Yuh shame chree nuh dead." Dr. G. was appointed from on High to be my natural othermother in the un-natural academic world of the doctoral program.

I didn't have to do research or teach for the entire first year of my fellowship. What? All I had to do was go to class, read the assigned readings, do the written responses and participate in class. I got this. It fit well with my program, which consisted of driving to Cleveland most weekends to see my baby girl and my family, plus hook up with my musician friends and do gigs in local Cleveland clubs. *This is true gravy.* Or so I thought, until Dr. G got wind of my version of the doctoral program.

"I've arranged summer funds for you. You'll be doing bibliographic work checkin sources for accuracy."

"Over the summah? Oh, I don't plan to be here over the summah, Dr. G I usually go home to Cleveland on weekends to see my baby, plus I do gigs and write songs with my musician friends."

"Say what? You sing, huh? I didn't know that, and I thought all of your daughters were living on campus with you?"

"Naw, I left the baby girl in Cleveland."

"What's his name?"

"What's whose name?"

"This fine brotha who got you driving back and forth to Cleveland every time you get a chance."

"I don't have a dude, Doc, I have to go see my daughter and plus I'll be doin my music."

"Okay. Yeah, I met your mom and your Godmother. You are blessed to have such a great support system. But check this out. You need to spend the summer up here and you need to put a freeze on nem weekend trips to Cleveland. Your baby'll be alright. It's not enough for you to do well in your courses. Your goal is to be one of the top scholars in the world on African American language and literacy. To be the best, you have to read every piece of scholarship that comes out. You have to stay in da library. You have to know the field like the back of your hand. Knowwhatumsayin? You cain't sing up on dis Ph.D. You have to read, write and research up on dis bad boy. Nah, sing up on dat."

Who in the hell did she thank she was? Sheeit, I'm 33 years old and have 3 kids of my own. I'm a grown-ass woman. I'll show her. I don't need her summah fundin. I'll find my own and I'll go to Cleveland whenever I want to.

As the summer months drew near, I answered an ad in the campus newspaper for a summer research assistant doing some editing as well as database searching. The pay was good and I could do the work from Cleveland. Perfect for my program. All I needed was a reference letter from Dr. G.

As the end of the semester approached, I needed to work closely with Dr. G to organize her upcoming courses for the next year for which I would be her teaching assistant. I also needed to pull my examination committee together. I'd heard horror stories of students who got stuck in doctoral programs because their committee members had huge differences in beliefs. Lore had it that it was best to let the major professor handpick the committee, to lessen the probability of a terrible experience.

All roads led to Dr. G. She was there to guide me through the maze of graduate school: which courses were right for me? Which professors would work well together to groom me? What would be my funding sources for professional development, summer living expenses? How do I handle myself as a conscious Black woman scholar in difficult situations with style and integrity?

I soon learned who Dr. G. was in my life. She was my othermother. Othermothers are a collective force of Black women engaged in the struggle to assist young Black people in overcoming obstacles[2]. She was nosy. She talked to me like a Black woman, in a way that gets under the skin and penetrates the soul. She told me where to get on and off. Even though she was never a street person, she respected street knowledge and used it as a point of

---

2   *Patricia Hill Collins 2000. Black Feminist Thought: Knowledge, Consciousness and the Politics of Empowerment. New York: Routledge.*

reference in teaching me the academic game. "Don't never forget where you came from. All you learned in the streets and in life, you need that. Don't think you can come up in here and chill. The academy can be foul, too. You gotta watch yo back in here, just like you had to watch your back out there." Dr. G skooled me in more ways than one.

Of course, the class I loved the most was Dr. G.'s Language Use in the African American Community. Each of the courses that I took throughout my doctoral journey helped me to study the question of Black folks and language from different angles: Concepts of Literacy; Theories and Histories of Composition; Language Policy; Sociolinguistics; Pragmatics/Speech Act Theory (how we are actually doing things with the words we use); Theories of Reading; Pedagogy as Knowledge Production. My goal became to end the lie that Black people have no intellectually worthy language and literacy traditions, that English and literacy are the same across different people and cultures, and that upper-class biased Whites in power and their followers (not all White people) get to define language and literacy for everyone else.

Leavin out and doggin out African American language and literacy traditions in education is accepted because "the powers that be" think Black students will not learn so-called Standardized English and how to think. Most of all, "the powers that be" have people thinking Black students will not be able to achieve important positions in society if African American language is respected. Ever since we were brought or bought into worlds, which we did not control, we have been educated to accept many teachings and mindsets that are not to our advantage.

It goes so much deeper than stereotypes: "the parents are lazy," "the parents don't care," "those students do not hear proper language at home," "they are illiterate," and "they have no culture." Our language did not put us in poverty. Our language does not have power because we do not have power. These ideas turned me on. I wanted to make a contribution to my culture and to the world of ideas.

Dr. G was right. In order to give back to my culture and my people, I had to do my best, learn all I could, read every study that dealt with language and literacy education of African Americans. My trips to Cleveland became few and far between. I practically lived in the library or in Dr. G.'s office. Although my children understood the importance of education, I often felt like an unfit mother. I went to their events and participated as best I could as a single parent, but my laptop was always right there, powered up. Even when I was supposed to be helping them with their homework, my own work was always on my mind. Sometimes I'd catch myself and try to push my work out of my mind so that I could really hear what they were saying to me and focus on them. We created our special time together—famba—that's when I locked away the laptop and focused on family time. With each course I took, I became totally immersed in academic life.

The next big step was exams. This was waay more intense than the Master's thesis oral exam. By this time, I had taken courses from my committee professors and they all knew intimately of my research interests and coursework. We worked together to generate a list of articles and books that I needed to read to become an expert in the areas of composition studies, applied linguistics and literacy studies.

After a set period of time, the committee made questions based on the literature I had to review to write my dissertation. These questions also helped me to develop research theories and methods. The first exam was three take-home questions to answer over the weekend. Thank God one of my classmates, a nice White lady named Cynthia, volunteered to let my girls spend the weekend at her house, because I barely got a wink of sleep the entire weekend. I sat at the computer pouring over my reading lists, books and articles, typing and editing and rewriting, walking back and forth to the refrigerator, hoping that another glass of kool-aid, a pickle, or a sandwich would help me think or write something better.

I drifted in and out of consciousness, a sweaty mess, until Cynthia brought the girls home Monday morning. But the sounds from their singing "mahmeeee" gave me the strength to press on. I was very happy that I was only asked to revise one question. Dr. G felt that I could do better, and I was given 24 hours to do so, and I did. The next round of exams allowed me to turn in a paper over a 4-week period. That was a lot less stressful, and I passed without having to revise anything. (Yay!)

For my dissertation research, I took all of the slave narratives, autobiographies, essays, novels, folk sayings, songs, rhymes, and Black writing or talk that I read or experienced and looked for the special insights that all of these showed about Black people and our views of life and how we created patterns in our writing and speech. I also looked at literature and oral traditions thought to belong to White people and their ancestors, those traditions that are taught in school that have been standardized by those in positions of power. Teaching and comparing both together, my goal was to value the styles and experiences of Black people and to apply what I learned from Carter G. Woodson, that not teaching Black people about ourselves is a form of miseducation. In order to teach the course, I had to have my proposal approved by the head of the English department. Luckily, Dr. G. had juice. She schooled me on how to write the proposal. She worked her magic on the department head, and the course was approved. I actually needed a majority of African American students to take the course, which was a bit of a challenge in a Big Ten, historically White university, but we made it happen.

The course dealt with racism, inequality, Black cultural identities, and most crucially, how all of this is wound up in being Black and literate.[3] Teaching this course taught me so much more than I ever thought it would. It was very challenging. So many things that Black people went through in earlier eras still plagued us, ideas about Black people and Black culture being less valuable popped up all the time. We thought a lot about what it meant to be miseducated and what it truly means to be literate. I wanted my students to feel good about writing, to be honest about our ideas, to take our writing and thinking to another level. Some students admitted that even though the course content was important what they were learning would not be valued anywhere else in the university or the world. And they were grateful for the opportunity to have studied the content. So many students get stripped of their writing and creative potential in college and even before coming to college.

I began presenting my ideas at writing and language conferences and professors from other schools started to approach

---

3   More information about the course is discussed in my book, African American Literacies 2002. New York & London: Routledge.

me almost immediately asking me to apply to their school for assistant professor positions. That definitely got my attention. Although my girls and I had enough to get by and we were"safe" in a university community, I had been a broke poor student now for quite a few years; but Dr. G told me not to pursue any job offers until I finished my dissertation. A lot of students never finish their Ph.D.'s because they take jobs early. Dr. G said I'd be able to write my own ticket if I stuck it out and wrote the best dissertation I could. And that's what I did.

Under her guidance, I went on to graduate with a Ph.D. in English from Michigan State University and Geneva Smitherman's African American Language and Literacy program, with a specialization in Composition and Applied Linguistics in 1996.

In 1996, I was recruited to the University of Minnesota's General College for my first job as an Assistant Professor of Composition. I felt like I was living a dream and that somebody was gonna pop up and tell my new employers about my past. So, I figured I'd do the honors.

"Terry, I am a former prostitute and I used to be on drugs," I blurted out to my new boss who was the director of Academic Affairs. I am who I am. I never wanted to put on airs and make myself out to be someone who I wasn't. I'm a girl from down the way, an ex-junkie, ex-ho, a baby mama, and I'm still just as good as anybody else on this planet.

Totally unphazed, he smiled and said, "Well, shit, welcome to Minnesota. Half the population is in recovery. You'll fit right in. I have a friend I'd like you to meet. She and her mom were both on the streets and they are struggling to stay straight. You'd be a big inspiration to them." Dayum! Terry was the coolest old hippy in the world. He was politically and socially conscious. All of his work was about equality for oppressed people. The General

College was dedicated to multicultural education forreal. They wanted to be world leaders in education for diversity. I should have known that Dr. G wouldn't agree to let me go anywhere that wasn't cool.

Another thing that tripped me out about Minneapolis was I never knew so many (politically conscious *and* active) Black folks lived there. When I got there, activists from the community came to my office and introduced themselves to me and got me involved in community activities right away. I became the organizer for the African American Read In, putting on writing contests and cultural programs for Black history month. The Minnesota Humanities Center was very supportive of my work and funded several of my projects, including Da Real Deal on Ebonics Conference in 1998 after the so-called Ebonics Controversy. The conference brought together the community with some of the top Black language scholars in the world. As cold as it is, I couldn't believe how incredibly warm Minnesota was for my daughters and me. The girls attended a project-based public school with an open school philosophy. It wasn't perfect—no place is, but Minnesota was open to cultural diversity and new ways of thinking about literacy education.

Though I tried to put it out of my mind, it really bothered me that none of my daughters had a father to speak of. One day I decided to call Calvin and see if he wanted to make arrangements to be in our daughter's life. I figured we could work that out. After all, he was a good dude. I never really knew why we broke up. He just seemed to lose interest not long after I had the baby. After I moved to Michigan, he rarely called to ask about our daughter.

Now that I was a bonafide professional woman, surely he would want to be involved with our child.

"Hey, it's Elaine. Remember me? The other girl you had a kid with?"

"Hey girl, how's everything going up there in Iceland? How they treatin you?"

"They treatin me good. Iceland is nice. They even have Black folks up here."

"Good. Good."

"... I'm comin to Cleveland for Thanksgiving and I wondered if you wanted to see your daughter. You haven't called or anything. Don't you wanna be in her life? She's a nice little girl. You'd love her."

"I know."

"How come you never call? I've never asked you for anything. I don't need your money or nothin, I just want you to be a man and be a father to your kid."

"I don't have a problem with that."

"Okay, well, I'll call you when I'm in town and you can come and pick her up or whatever."

"Okay, call me."

Sure enough, I buzzed him while we were in Cleveland on Thanksgiving break. Just like he promised, he came and picked her up and took her with him to his family's home for a whole day. He even took her shopping and bought her some nice outfits and some Black baby dolls. I remember how happy she was when they returned that evening. They were holding hands and she called to me as my mom opened the door for them.

"Maaahmee, come see me and my daddy!" I was so happy for her. My daddy loved the ground I walked on when I was growing up, so I was happy way down deep inside for her. Daddy-daughter connections are crucial.

"Say goodbye to daddy. He'll call you and come back to see you again."

"Bye daddy."

"Bye baby girl," said Calvin as he hugged her, exchanged waves with her and headed out of the house. I had no idea of the meaning of that goodbye.

A few weeks later, I got a letter from Calvin's lawyer about verifying paternity. *What*? How in the hell could he fix his mouth to ask me to take a paternity test? I called him and gave him a piece of my mind.

"Oh, so that's what this is all about? That's why you don't never call or make no arrangements to see her? You don't think she yours. Okay. I'll take the test and I'll get child support, too. How about dat? Mr. I Wanna Do the Right Thing." *Bamm!* I slammed the phone on his ass.

My daughter and I went to a local DNA testing center and gave samples. They took pictures of us and Calvin did the same thing at a facility in Cleveland. A few weeks later, I got the news: There was a less than 1% chance that Calvin was my daughter's father. What? I hadn't been with anyone else. Oh, hell to the naw. It's a mistake somewhere. I called everybody involved and went back over the results. Nope. The test is foolproof. Calvin is not the father. I never laugh at them women on Maury. That shit ain't nowhere near funny.

So many nights I tossed and turned in my bed combing my brain cells over. Now when did I get pregnant? I rehearsed what had happened in the time when Calvin returned to me from Georgia. I stopped seeing Chris when Calvin got back. I loved Calvin. I didn't intentionally lie on him—but I must have gotten pregnant by Chris! By now, Chris had settled himself down and was married and living in California, I heard. His cousin lived right across the street from our Cleveland house, so I did know how to get in touch with him. Dayum! I got Chris' cell phone number from his cousin. How do you fix your mouth to ask a brotha to take a DNA test?

I didn't. I just made small talk and tried to find out the next time he would be in Cleveland. I scheduled our next visit to coincide with his. Sure enough, Chris came through just like he said he would. We sat on my porch and reminisced about the good ole days at CSU and our little rendezvous.

"Speaking of how we useta do. You know, I thought my baby girl's father was this other dude's. After all these years, I found out, he ain't her dad."

"What? That's messed up."

"The only other person I was with around that time was you."

"You bullshittin."

"I shit you not."

"What year was dat?"

"1991."

"Hey, you know I'm married now and my wife just had a baby. What if she is mines?"

"Look, I don't want nothin from you. I don't need your money. The Lord is blessin me. I just want my daughter to know her dad. She is nice and pretty and you will love her."

We went inside my house and I called to my baby girl and told her it was time to get her hair combed. Chris' hair was soft and curly and so was hers. Chris was tall and skinny and so was she. He stared at her. Felt her hair as I braided it.

"She might be. She's very pretty."

"Yes, she is."

We shifted our conversation back to his life in California and how good I still looked. Chit chat and bullshit. When I finished

• 243 •

my daughter's hair, I walked him to the door. He asked me what I wanted to do. I suggested that we go for DNA testing. I assured him that I didn't want money, that I didn't want him, or to mess up his life with his wife and kid. We exchanged cell phone numbers and email addresses. Though I tried to contact him, I haven't seen or heard from him since. I guess he is happily ever after in Cali. I just told my daughter the truth: The man who I thought was your daddy ain't. What else could I do? I sho ain't goin on Maury!

Being on tenure track is stressful enough. Tenure track is when the university signs you up for a job—but you are really temporary. They make sure you meet their criteria of being a scholar in whatever your field is before they make a permanent place for you. It is based on how many articles and or books you publish with presses that are respected in your field. Sometimes it is based on your ability to be awarded grants from foundations or the federal government. It all depends on your field, your department, and how many haters are judging you. With all of this stress, I didn't need no baby daddy drama.

I focused on my academic life. I hoped that my achievements in this new world would erase the pain of my old world. In the world of what they call the Research One University, your value is based on your ability to create theories, solve social problems, publish your results with respected presses and research journals, and become internationally known on the microphone. From a business perspective, nobody cares about your personal struggles. But more were to come.

The next time I came home to Cleveland, I noticed that things were changing. Our house wasn't neat. There were no groceries to speak of in the cupboards or fridge. Mama and Daddy looked a lot more frail. It was the first time that I realized that Mama and Daddy wouldn't be with me forever. I got angry at my brother who lived in the downstairs apartment.

"How come this house is like dis? Cain't you help keep this place up? Ain't hardly no food in here."

"You da girl. Ain't nobody tell you to get no job in Minnesota! You couldn't get no job at Cleveland State? I do help around here. Who you think take out the trash, mow the lawn, shovel the snow, and give Daddy a bath?"

"Give Daddy a bath?"

That made things plain. I spent the rest of my visit cleaning, cooking, and shopping for food and household supplies.

"Mama, if something happen to you and Daddy, I don't know what I'ma do."

"Chzzzz." Mama sucked her teeth. "How you mean, if someting hap'm. You mean WHEN we die. I know what you gwan do. Mi ago put dis house inna fe yuh an yuh bruddah nyehm. I don't owe a living ass a cent pon disya house. You gonna tek cyere of da girls and you and your brother gonna keep dis house." Mama made my brother and me go to the bank with her. She took all of her savings and Daddy's savings out of their names and gave it to us and put the house in our names. I was still in denial.

"Mama I don't know why you doin all this now. Y'all ain't goin nowhere no time soon."

Sure enough during my work at the University of Minnesota, Mama and Daddy's health continued to fail and regular travel back and forth to Cleveland, Ohio, from Minneapolis, Minnesota, was a far and expensive plane ride. Just as I began to worry about being so far away from Ohio, I got a call from Keith Gilyard, a colleague, who explained to me that he recommended me to the

English Department at Pennsylvania State University, as someone with a specialization in African American Rhetoric. Keith was a good friend of Dr. G.'s. We met years before at one of our professional conferences while I was a grad student, and he knew that I wanted to live and teach in Ohio or New York City. NYC was one of my dream locations since I was a singer-songwriter, and Ohio—well, there's just no place like home.

"Keif, what's African American Rhetoric?"

"Just go to Penn State and drop your research on 'em," said Keith. Shortly thereafter, I was asked to deliver a lecture to Penn State's English department. I got a call from a dude by the name of Jack. He said that I was highly recommended by Keith and that if we found ourselves compatible that I would love living and working in the prestigious environment of Penn State.

Giving a talk to PSU's English department wasn't that threatening. Heck, by then I had talked to room after room full of White folk about African American Language and Literacy education. Not only did I talk about African American Language, I spoke it in my lecture. Going on a job talk is a piece of cake when you already have a good job and you don't need it. I said everything I felt like saying and the way I felt comfortable saying it. After my lecture, one of the two brothers in the room, came up to me and shook my hand, introducing himself: "Hey sista, enjoyed your lecture. I'm Clyde Woods."

He gave me his card and left. I thought to myself about the barren land that Penn State must be…hardly any Black folks. Why in the world would they want to hire me?

Minneapolis made more sense—large African immigrant population. "Large" urban African American population. Come to find out, just like every other major historically White institution, Penn State had to try to enhance their ability to attract and keep

Black faculty and students. By hiring people like Keith and me, they hoped to put some flavah in their environment and become known for having top scholars of diverse backgrounds.

In a few short weeks, I was offered a hefty salary increase to open up shop in "Happy Valley." Not long after I got to campus, while walking on the quad one day, I spotted the brotha who gave me his card at my job talk.

"Yo, Clyde. It's me, Elaine Richardson," I called to him.

Clyde ran over to me: "Sista, you mean to tell me they hired you wit all that stuff you was saying IN EBONICS."

We both cracked up. "Yes they did."

It worked out for my life at the time because living in Pennsylvania gave me the opportunity to be closer to Cleveland. In 1998, I accepted the position, and I am glad that I did especially because I was able to drive home from State College, PA to Cleveland, Ohio every other weekend to clean, cook and shop for my parents.

One day I got a call from Mama saying that Daddy had fallen out of the bed during the night and when she found him the next morning, she thought he was dead. He was ice cold and disoriented. Mama just cried. It broke my heart. Mama and Daddy weren't the lovey dubby type of couple. Remember the lifelong fight they had? This was the day it ended. Mama catered to Daddy like I had never seen before. After he spent a few days in the hospital, they told Mama that Daddy shouldn't live at home anymore. His Alzheimer's had reached the point where she couldn't manage him. Daddy moved to a nursing home and Mama began to come and stay with me.

Sometimes she would visit with us for one or two weeks; but she never would agree to move in with me. She and I were Daddy's only visitors, so she couldn't be away from Cleveland too long. Plus she always said "Two big ooman cyan stay inna one house." Mama still loved to smoke her cigarettes. And, I was strict about making her eat right. My brother let her eat and smoke the way she wanted while she was in Cleveland. So after I would start to get on her nerves about her smoking and eating, she'd demand that I take her back to her own house.

One day when I came to Cleveland to pick Mama up, her spunk was gone.

"Mama, won't you just stay with me in State College? I promise, we'll go see Daddy often. Okay?"

"Okay," she said with quiet compliance. I couldn't believe my ears.

I packed up all Mama's things and she moved to State College with me. The next week, a colleague Cindy Selfe asked me to give a talk on Hiphop Literacies and technology in Florida for the National Council of Teachers of English.

Right after I gave my talk, my oldest daughter called me. I could barely get her to calm down, so I could understand what she was saying.

"Mommy, granny on the floor and she cain't talk!"

"Did you call 911?"

"No, I just called you."

I told my poor little 15 year-old daughter to call 911 and that I would get home as soon as I could.

Oh my God. I nearly passed out. I panicked. I called Pastor McKenzie, Sherren Gilyard, Charlotte Carraway, my dearest friends in State College and they all rushed to the hospital to be with Mama until I could get there. Mama had a major stroke. Thankfully, Mama didn't die. The doctor said that Mama needed the constant around the clock care of a nursing home. I was cool with that. She was right there with me in State College and I could go see her every day. Now, both Daddy and Mama were in nursing homes. I never thought that would happen.

I went back and forth to Cleveland a couple times a month to see Daddy, but the home attendants knew that he didn't have anyone to visit him except me. They didn't take good care of him. One time when I went to see Daddy he sat there in his mess the whole visit. I begged the attendants to please clean him up for me and they took their time until they got good and damn ready to clean him, even though I reported them to a supervisor. I felt so helpless.

One Friday morning I got a call from the nursing home doctor. He said that he didn't think Mama would make it through the weekend. *What? How you know? You ain't none of God*, I thought. When I visited Mama that day, she looked so tired. She was breathing real hard but she could nod her head—yes or no—to answer my questions sometimes. I would sit with Mama for a while and then go home and work for a couple hours. I did notice that Mama couldn't seem to clear her lungs. When I looked in her mouth it was full of phlegm.

I washed my hands and stuck one hand in Mama's mouth to help clear out her throat with tissue. I told one of the nurses that I didn't like how hard she was breathing and she went and put Mama on some oxygen. Just around this time, my daughter called for a ride home from the teen dance. Mama couldn't seem to keep her eyes open, but she still seemed responsive. I held open Mama's eyes and told her that I was going to pick up Ebony from the dance and that I'd be right back. It looked like she nodded okay.

As soon as I got my daughter in the house, the nurse was on the phone saying that I should rush back. When I got back, Mama was gone. I couldn't believe it. Mama was gone. She didn't look dead. Her body was still warm, but she wasn't struggling to breathe anymore. I felt angry at the nurses. They should have told me that I shouldn't have left. I wanted to be there for Mama like she had been there for me. That was in March of 2000. Daddy died three months later.

Mama's sister, my Auntie Fodie, came from Jamaica to visit me. She felt sorry for me that I lost my Mama. Auntie did everything for me that she knew Mama would have done—cooked, cleaned, prayed for me, while I spent many nights in my office or somewhere glued to a laptop, writing and reading.

In 2003, I published my first scholarly book, *African American Literacies*. In 2004, I was granted tenure at Pennsylvania State University, and I was named a Fulbright Research/Lecturer to the University of the West Indies for comparative studies in Afro-American and Afro-Jamaican oral traditions. Also in 2004, one of my co-edited collections, *Understanding African American Rhetoric: Classical Origins to Contemporary Innovations* was awarded the National Communication Association's 2004 most outstanding book. In 2005, my book *African American Literacies* won the National Reading Conference's Edward Fry Book Award for Outstanding Research in Literacy Studies. My second single authored book *Hiphop Literacies* was published in 2006. In 2007, I won Cleveland State University's Distinguished Alumni Award for Outstanding Contributions to the Profession, the Community and Cleveland State University. Also, in 2007, The Ohio State University awarded me tenure as a full professor of Literacy Studies. I've given talks all over the nation, in the UK, Canada, the Caribbean.

I am still healing after all these years. I am learning to love and accept myself and to keep growing. I am figuring out how to put all of the pieces of me together and use them in my teaching, research, community work and in my music. I use my life to mentor, mother, and sister others. God saved me for this. We can't give up. We have to keep fighting for our voices to be heard, to save ourselves and our children, from miseducation, and spiritual death.

If I am worth anything, it's because of Mama. Mama always let me back in the house. Mama kept my oldest daughter for me when I was a po ho on dope. Mama's stories about how she wished she had an oppachunity to finish school in Jamaica, of how her father died when she was 13, and of how she was taken out of school to work by Grandma saved my life. Those stories planted the shame chree in me to remind me that my life is not my own.

CPSIA information can be obtained
at www.ICGtesting.com
Printed in the USA
FFHW022159161219
57027073-62633FF